ADLARD
COLES
MANUAL

UPGRADING YOUR BOAT'S INTERIOR

MIKE WESTIN

ADLARD COLES NAUTICAL
LONDON

Published by Adlard Coles Nautical
an imprint of Bloomsbury Publishing Plc
50 Bedford Square, London, WC1B 3DP
www.adlardcoles.com

Copyright © Michael Westin 2011.
First published in Sweden by Columbus Förlag and
Praktiskt Båtägande.
Published in the UK in 2012 by Adlard Coles Nautical.

ISBN 978-1-4081-3295-1

A CIP catalogue record for this book is available from the
British Library.

This book is produced using paper that is made from
wood grown in managed, sustainable forests. It is natural,
renewable and recyclable. The logging and manufacturing
processes conform to the environmental regulations of the
country of origin.

Translation by Marie Allen.
Series design by James Watson.
Page layout by Susan McIntyre.
Typeset in URWGrotesk.
Printed and bound in China by C&C Offset Printing Co.

Note: While all reasonable care has been taken in
the publication of this book, the publisher takes no
responsibility for the use of the methods or products
described in this book.

The author wishes to thank: Jonas Arvidsson, Håkan
Arvidsson, July Auguststierna, Michael Christiansen,
Roine Falk, Lars Fjelddahl, Hanna Fristedt, Jenni Kasajima,
Ingegerd Lindén, Jakob Magnusson, Kim Rask,
Jan-G Westin, Björn Åqvist and a special thanks to the
boat owners that showed me their boats.

>> CONTENTS

>> HOW TO IMPROVE YOUR BOAT

A few years ago, a group of fellow enthusiasts and I started a boat magazine (the first new boat magazine in Sweden for over 20 years), with the aim of describing a range of practical projects, from tinkering with boat engines to making your own cabin cushions.

The special themed issues on boat interiors proved very popular, particularly the sections that were not just glossy 'at-home-with' articles, but demonstrated ways of improving your own boat.

When we first started gathering material for the articles, the various craftsmen were reluctant to reveal their trade secrets in our magazine – but they soon found themselves receiving more commissions, since not all boat owners wanted to carry out the work themselves, either because of lack of time or the belief that they do not possess the skills to do it.

And even those readers who didn't carry out their own improvement projects found it useful to know how it is done – it helped them to ask the right questions and to place a more coherent order. Quite simply, they became better customers, albeit more demanding!

My aim with this book is to show how you can make your boat more practical and at the same time more comfortable. This is a subject that appeals to me, since I spend a lot of time on boats. I have to admit that, with age, comfort becomes a higher priority. Camping in boats has its charm, but these days I enjoy mod cons such as a fridge and comfortable berths, even when moored in a far-away natural harbour.

Photo: Lars Fjelddahl

FUNCTIONALITY BEFORE FORM

Personally, I am not that interested in decor, and for me the emphasis is on function. It is fine for the improvements to look attractive, as long as functionality is not compromised. All the projects described in the book originate from a practical need to make life comfortable on board a leisure boat (in my case *Roobarb*, an 8-metre (27-ft) project boat used for long-distance sailing, where I spend weeks or months on board).

There are of course countless things to be said on the subject of interior design for boats, so I have limited myself to a few selective improvements below deck and in the cockpit. I have mainly used my own projects as a basis, since my view is that if I can do it, then most reasonably adept boat owners should be able to too.

Upgrading Your Boat's Interior aims to both inspire you to make changes and guide you through several projects, step by step. The two main projects consist of making new cushions from scratch and building a new fitted galley, with a worktop and improved storage.

I have also compiled some useful information on equipment and materials in the 'References' section at the end of the book.

I hope you find some projects you can use as they are outlined in this book, or that inspire similar improvement projects!

PRACTICAL CONSIDERATIONS

When planning this book, I had to decide what to do about prices and where to source the various materials. I am aware that a book could have a long shelf life, and I have as far as possible tried to avoid including too many prices and suppliers, which in some cases will come and go.

About Mike Westin

Mike Westin is a boating journalist whose love of sailing began at the tender age of ten. Not long after, he became a sailing instructor, sailing tall training ships and undertaking a couple of long-distance cruises under sail in Europe with small boats (6-8m/20-27ft) and a 15-month cruise in the South Seas.

Having finished a part-time three-year cruise in northern Europe, he is now an editor-in-chief for a popular boating magazine. A keen promoter of matters of safety on yachts, he is also a coxswain in his local lifeboat crew.

Mike has written a series of three books charting the restoration of *Roobarb*, a Vancouver 27 built in 1977: *Replacing Your Boat's Engine*, *Upgrading Your Boat's Interior* and *Replacing Your Boat's Electrical System*.

Roobarb, a Vancouver 27, before the rebuild started.

>> ABOUT THE PROJECT BOAT, A VANCOUVER 27

Americans call this type of small, long-distance boat a 'pocket cruiser', and it was in North America that Rob Harris constructed this Vancouver 27 in the late 1960s for a couple planning to cross the South Pacific from Canada to New Zealand. The boat type proved more than up to the task, and series production commenced a few years later. In total 250 of the type 27 were built, both in Canada and in England. A minor modification was made to the design in 1983, and about 60 of the Vancouver 28s were then produced and are still being traded.

THE PROJECT BOAT *ROOBARB*

The project boat *Roobarb* was built from a kit in 1977, and I purchased it 25 years later to use as a practical platform for the articles in the Swedish magazine *Practical Boat Owning*, launched in 2003.

This type of boat is not common in Sweden, but *Roobarb* displays most of the faults and flaws of 1970s boats and so is a very suitable candidate for a renovation and improvement project – from a new grooved teak deck to building a brand new galley. The eventual goal was to sail the boat long-distance, to show that you can do it on a limited budget.

The purpose of upgrading *Roobarb*'s interior was to make the boat more comfortable, modern and functional for long-distance sailing and for the weeks and months that I planned to live on board in a space the size of the average bathroom.

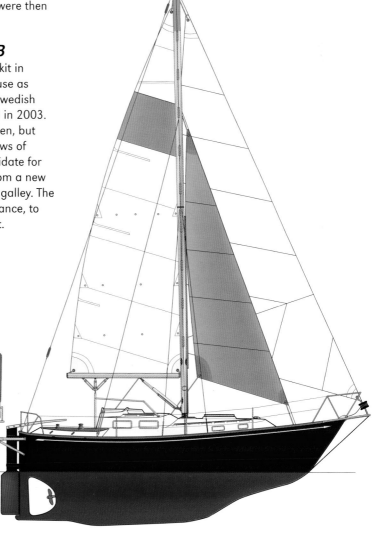

About the Vancouver 27

Length: *8.23 m (27 ft)*
Load waterline length: *6.99 m (23 ft)*
Beam: *2.66 m (8.75 ft)*
Draught: *1.30 m (4.25 ft)*
Displacement: *approx. 4.1 tonnes (just over 5 tonnes loaded)*
In the hull: *1.6 tonnes lead*
Sail area: *35.2 m² (378 sq ft)*
Engine: *Vetus M3.09 25 hp*
Fuel: *245 litres (54 gal)*
Water: *approx. 100 litres (22 gal)*
Builders: *Northshore/kit*

While the layout of an old and new boat remains fairly similar, today there are many improvements using modern materials and furnishings. This is an IW31 from the 1970s.

01

INSPIRATION

>> DEVELOPMENT IN PROGRESS

Boat owners are traditionalists – at times almost retro enthusiasts, it seems! Or perhaps it is only boatbuilders who believe that we, the boat owners, are like that, since the layout of leisure boats today looks virtually the same as it did in the 1960s but is more aesthetically pleasing.

The fact that our boats are still so similar today to those built in the 1960s is mostly a positive thing, because it means that a functional basic interior design has been found that maximises the boat's internal space. There have been very few functional innovations in this field.

By far the most common design is a forepeak with a V-shaped berth, followed by a saloon with two berths opposite each other and a folding table in the middle, or sometimes a dinette, a linear or L-shaped galley, the heads by the steps, or maybe one or two berths and an after cabin.

Of course, newer, wider and more box-like boat shapes provide considerably more internal space and include, for example, large double berths under the cockpit, even in smaller boats 6–8 m (20–26 ft) in length and improved facilities.

The 'styling' trend now seems to have reached the boating world, just as it did with cars 10–15 years ago. The producers want to sell not just a boat but also a lifestyle, and I believe that this trend will grow rapidly in the near future.

There is a huge difference in the aesthetics of a classic mahogany interior from the 1970s (see opposite) and the highly polished interior of the Fjord 40 (above). The prevailing trend is gradually moving towards the latter style, as consumer tastes change from the traditional to the sleek and modern.

ENVIRONMENTAL CHOICE

A positive aspect of development is that hardwoods are used far less in interior furnishing today. This is environmentally sound, because the rainforest where these extremely slow-growing types of wood are found has been devastated.

Boat owners are gradually beginning to accept other, more local and less threatened types of wood – cherry and other 'pale' European woods are becoming more and more common, which of course is progress. To learn more about wood and its characteristics, see Chapter 7.

Plastic and composite materials are also becoming more common – and plastic does not look as dull as it did 20 years ago.

INSPIRATION

In this book there are several examples of good (and sometimes not so good) interior solutions.

But let's start with some history. On the next page we will travel almost a century back in time when we look at how two enthusiasts salvaged an old mahogany cruiser and restored it virtually to its original state.

It is plain to see that development really has progressed, not only in terms of materials but also in function.

But has everything truly improved?

The boat exterior has not been forgotten – this is a two-tone Bavaria 44. It is possible that mass-produced boats will soon have 'optional extras' to personalise them, just like cars with tinted windows, leather seats and cool aluminium wheel trims.

The French boatbuilder Harmony makes bright, airy interiors. This 10-m (34-ft) boat attracted a good deal of attention when it first came on the market.

>> CLASSIC INTERIOR

The motor yacht *Atala* was built from mahogany in 1916 in Sweden. She has been carefully renovated to be as true to the original as possible.

When the boat was found in 1989 in the Göta River in Sweden she was in very poor condition – the old engine barely survived the journey back to her new berth in Stockholm.

The current owners dismantled m/y *Atala* and spent almost every hour of three years renovating her. Another two or three guys helped out in their spare time.

'It was a long-held dream of having a real yacht that took shape,' says owner Johan Winquist. 'But it was a real drain on our finances.'

The restoration cost the owners between £300,000 and £400,000. The aim was to recreate the former elegance, sticking as close to the original as possible. Although a few of the original details were salvaged, virtually the whole interior has been remade, using the old interior as a template. Only a few drawers survive from the original interior from 1916, and these too have been given a new veneer front.

The saloon on board the motor yacht Atala *is close to the original. The table can seat eight to ten people.*

BETTER THAN THE ORIGINAL

The same materials and dimensions have been used; the biggest change is that solid mahogany deck beams have replaced the original steel deck beams.

'The boat is better than the original. The development of materials and craftsmanship has come a long way, and we have of course made use of that,' says Johan.

The interior, which took almost two years to renovate, is made of solid mahogany, with plenty of brass details to create that distinctive early 20th century atmosphere on board.

In order to restore the exterior, the new owners traced the original photographs in the archives of the Maritime Museum in Stockholm, which they used as a master for some of the reconstruction, such as the chimney.

M/y *Atala* was originally commissioned by bank director R. Bovin, but has since been owned by Torsten Kreuger and John Henry Sager, among others.

Atala under her protective wooden roof at Pampas Marina in Solna, Stockholm, protecting the wood from dangerous UV rays.

Right: Like the rest of the boat, the heads cubicle is built from solid mahogany.

Atala

Length: *18.5 m (60 ft)*
Beam: *3.6 m (12 ft)*
Draught: *1.3 m (4.25 ft)*
Weight: *18 tonnes*
Engine: *250 hp Cummins*
Other info: *renovated 1989–92*

Above: A traditional kerosene lantern in the skylight window casts a warm glow over the cabin.

Left: There are two single berths in the aft cabin.

>> THE FUTURE

On board the motorboat Fjord 40, designed by the German boatbuilder Hanse Yachts, we get a glimpse of what we can soon expect to become standard. Forms and shapes based on both home interior design and the extremely competitive automotive industry are becoming more common in the boating world.

The Fjord 40, launched at the 2007 Düsseldorf Boat Show, has a very clean interior dominated by large areas of glass, earthy tones, square shapes and large deck areas with no difference in level, making it easy to move around on the boat.

The interior design is by Mark Tucker of Design Unlimited in England. He describes his interior as 'reduced to the max' by providing top-quality essential comforts. This is still very unusual for mass-produced boats.

The wide hull, by the Swiss-based design company Allseas, also stands out from the crowd because of its angular shape and straight stem. The company has also designed sailing boats (for other manufacturers) with essentially the same lines.

>> THE CREATION OF A NEW INTERIOR

As part of her undergraduate degree in industrial design, Hanna Fristedt designed interiors for a forthcoming Maxi sailing boat and also gave a facelift to an older Nimbus motorboat. Here she shows us how to create an interior where functionality is the keyword.

All good design projects start with finding out about the 'end user' – in this case, whom the interior is going to suit and what practical criteria should be fulfilled. Boatbuilders generally have a good idea of who their customers are, but Hanna carries out her own in-depth interviews with various boat owners to learn more about the problems they experience and what

improvements they would like to see in their interiors. On the project for the Maxi boatbuilders, Hanna worked on planning and decorating the cabins, heads and shower rooms.

'It is important to find the right design and materials that suit the company's profile and always keep the target group's needs in focus,' Hanna says.

In the bulkheads between the various spaces, Hanna has fitted panels of milky-white Plexiglass, which lets in light from the skylight and lighting, breaks up the dark mahogany, and provides brightness, while preserving privacy.

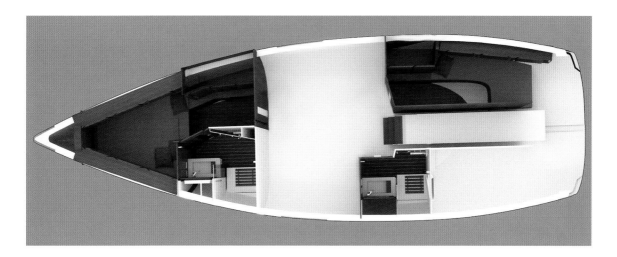

The Maxi boat is a forthcoming model, which will be about 11.5 m (38 ft). Maxi boats are series-produced on the island of Gotland, and all phases of the production need to run smoothly. The interior must be simple and cost-effective to construct, and yet easy for boatbuilders to fit into the space on board.

FIRST DRAWINGS

After analysing the requirements it is time to make drawings, which are presented to a working group at the boatbuilders. The group selects one or two of the ideas to develop and Hanna starts by building a few simple physical models to get a feel for the space. At the same time she makes three-dimensional computer images, which give a clearer picture of how the interior will look from various angles, as well as enabling Hanna to assess materials.

Full-scale models of the interior are constructed out of cardboard boxes, chairs and other materials, with tape on the floor to show the external dimensions of the boat. The models help Hanna to get an idea of space, functionality and dimensions. She maintains that it is imperative to get a feel for the practical functionality of a design, and how easy it will be to move through the space. It can be difficult to imagine if working only from computerised 3D programs. But from this software, Hanna can create photo-realistic images that will give the project group a clear view of how the final result may look.

Detailed planning for the spaces that Hanna worked on for the project, plus the main bulkheads, which face in towards the saloon. There are heads on the port side and a cabin on the starboard stern. An alternative plan is to replace the heads by a further cabin in the stern with berths. The empty space in the middle was a project for another design group.

The first drawings with Hanna's initial ideas for how a new interior can be created.

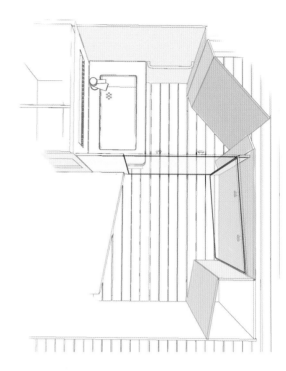

Good storage is a top priority in the cabins. Between the berths, pull-out panels can be used as seats or to make a double berth.

Below, left to right: Hanna builds models of the interior from boxes and board to enable her to test dimensions and functionality.

Above: A preliminary layout drawing of a heads cubicle. Behind the bulkhead, with the sink made of composite material, is a wet locker for foul weather gear.

FINAL ADJUSTMENTS

When Hanna has finished the design work, but before final approval by the boatyard, she and the engineers and production heads go through all the parts and components involved, make amendments and adjust dimensions, before the final result is ready for production.

Then it is over to a design engineer, who transforms Hanna's 3D drawings into CAD (computer-aided design) drawings to be used for the production of the various units.

But before a boat is launched on the market, there will be additional input from others to areas of the interior and to the hull – in total, it takes anywhere between several months and a couple of years from the initial idea to a boat being launched on the market.

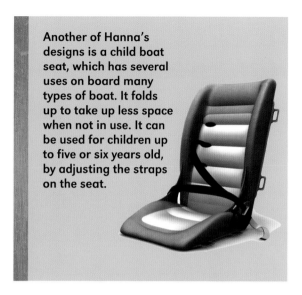

Another of Hanna's designs is a child boat seat, which has several uses on board many types of boat. It folds up to take up less space when not in use. It can be used for children up to five or six years old, by adjusting the straps on the seat.

In a previous project to renovate the galley on a Nimbus 300R, Hanna created a new galley, with a built-in bar and a special unit for storing crockery neatly. Lights were fitted behind the Plexiglass doors to make it easier to find things in the cabinets, as well as making the interior brighter.

This shows the working model (left), with Hanna trying out the galley for herself, and the completed project (right).

>> ROOBARB'S NEW INTERIOR

Of course, nothing is 'perfect' for everyone! Every boat is a compromise in one way or another. Boat interiors are also often hard to change a great deal – the interior is probably already arranged in the best possible way, as established by the original designer. But minor changes can make a big difference.

The renovation jobs on *Roobarb* have been both large and small, from installing a new engine and replacing the electrical system to projects that mainly revolved around making the boat more comfortable to spend time in. Most of the projects in this book fall into the latter category.

TAKING A SAW TO THE INTERIOR

Roobarb was a rather rundown 1970s boat, built as a kit by a boat owner who was practical, but far from professional. This, of course, made it easier to undertake major changes – taking a saw to a boat built by a proper yard may not feel quite as easy.

The cockpit leads straight into the galley. This has been painted mostly white and we have chosen bright orange and cornflower blue accessories. The galley has been renovated and the front decorated with a text in vinyl.

All cushions on board have covers made from a sun-proof, mould-resistant, dirt- and water-repellent Italian fabric called Tempotest, here in a bold bright orange.

The previous owner had in some respects tailored the interior to his own requirements, with the intention of using the boat for long-distance sailing some day. The original design drawings only allowed for two or three berths in this boat type, to suit a couple sailing the seas; consequently, there is plenty of space for a galley and storage, considering the boat is only just 8 m (27 ft) long.

The dream of long-distance sailing lived on when I started planning the optimal use of surfaces and storage areas.

Necessity sparks ideas, and I think that is a rather enjoyable aspect of improvement projects – when ideas need to be generated and the right equipment and accessories located, in order to find the best solution for a new design.

But most boats already have a reasonably functional interior fitted by the boatyard, which is in most cases good enough to work in the future as well. But sometimes solutions do not work in the way they were initially planned.

MORE LIGHT

Our primary objective was to have more light in the cabin – so with the help of some tins of paint, a composite board, some plywood pieces, teak veneer and brightly coloured new textiles, Jenni Kasajima (the interior stylist) and I set out to transform *Roobarb* into a more modern and attractive boat.

Colours and textiles are always easy to change, so don't be afraid to repaint after a few years if you want something different, or have just tired of it.

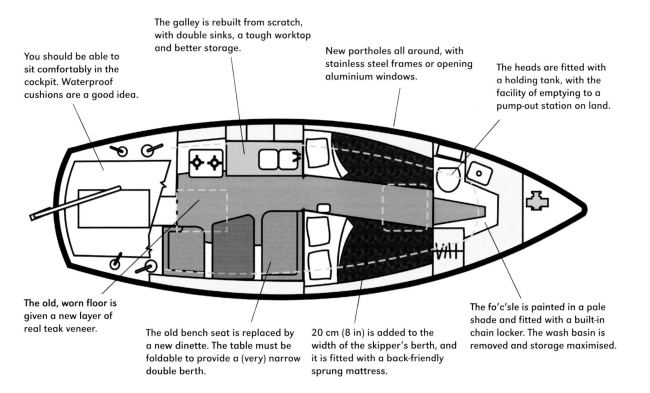

The galley is rebuilt from scratch, with double sinks, a tough worktop and better storage.

You should be able to sit comfortably in the cockpit. Waterproof cushions are a good idea.

New portholes all around, with stainless steel frames or opening aluminium windows.

The heads are fitted with a holding tank, with the facility of emptying to a pump-out station on land.

The old, worn floor is given a new layer of real teak veneer.

The old bench seat is replaced by a new dinette. The table must be foldable to provide a (very) narrow double berth.

20 cm (8 in) is added to the width of the skipper's berth, and it is fitted with a back-friendly sprung mattress.

The fo'c'sle is painted in a pale shade and fitted with a built-in chain locker. The wash basin is removed and storage maximised.

The galley (above) and dining area (right) on board Roobarb, *before the renovation.*

Over a couple of years, I have carried out a series of projects for the boat's interior. The biggest individual task was to build a new galley and dining area, where it was really a question of ripping it out and starting from scratch.

A NEW SURFACE

Many heavy objects had been dropped on the old mahogany floor. Instead of buying new, expensive marine plywood flooring, I chose to treat the old floor with (almost as expensive) teak veneer. The result was both attractive and non-slip.

The biggest impact on the appearance was sanding down all the mahogany plywood in the cabin and painting it a light colour, which really made the boat feel much more spacious.

In the sleeping area to the front of the boat, the biggest change is that I made new, comfortable berth mattresses with proper sprung pockets. These days I sleep better in the boat than I do at home (see also Chapter 3).

The cushions were covered in a tough, white cloth. White is perhaps not the most practical colour on a long-distance sailing boat, but when necessary it is easy to repaint, recover cushions, or cut a new rug for the floor.

The cockpit can be turned into a berth. Jenni has used the cushions to make a bed for a romantic night under the stars. The material for the sleeping pads is water-resistant, and we covered it in the same sun-proof, mould-resistant fabric we used for the rest of the boat.

TIP FOR PAINTING

A good tip is to use water-based two-component epoxy emulsion, perfect for boat interiors with its hard, waterproof, glossy coat.

This type of paint is normally included in the manufacturer's trade product range, but can also be purchased in relatively small quantities and could be a possible alternative to an alkyd paint, well-known to DIY-users.

It is available in white (gloss and matt), and costs around £200 for 5 litres.

BRIGHT COLOURS

The boat interior stylist Jenni had many suggestions as to how to improve the interior on board *Roobarb*. The idea was to break away from the ordinary a little, and dare to try something new. One main objective was also to make the interior lighter by choosing pale textiles and bright colours that reflect light into the boat.

Jenni did a great job, which in part remained on board after the photos of the new interior were taken. I have kept some of the orange cushions and all the floral textiles (Fig Leaves from Tempotest), which are Teflon-coated and weather- and windproof. There are three colours (white, pale green and orange) with the same pattern everywhere in the boat.

More about Jenni's interior work on the next page.

⟩⟩ THE STYLIST'S TASK

The boat interior stylist Jenni Kasajima was involved in giving *Roobarb* a facelift. Here she describes in her own words what she thought and did when she created the style for the boat.

I find it is the unusual and unexpected that make surroundings interesting, provided it is done with feeling. That is why it was especially fun to create this interior together with Mike, because we both lack restrictions and we are totally uninhibited when it comes to breaking with convention.

UNTRENDY

It is important to try to figure out what you really like and not what is 'trendy'. Trendy will always become unfashionable with time, and you easily tire of what you have not chosen according to your own heart and mind; although really there is no such thing as a trend in boat interiors – not yet, unless you call all the blue-green and off-white textiles a trend. In that case, this trend has lasted a very long time, and we can live with it because we are only on board the boat for a limited period of time each year.

UNTRADITIONAL

But Mike and I – with due respect to all who love the solid wood feel, and who want to preserve the boat exactly the way it is – want to inspire those readers who have grown tired of the conventional and are not afraid to try something new. All boats have their possibilities and their owners, and if you have a beautiful old wooden boat, you should of course preserve the original style if you love the way it is. If, on the other hand, you have an old, boring and worn boat, it may be fun to give it a proper facelift. And if the wood has become a bit dull, it is even easier to throw caution to the wind and paint or do something else exciting.

Jenni runs the interior styling company Seabreeze, and she likes to be hands-on.

When Jenni was selecting textiles and furnishings, she did a few tests with different colour combinations through image manipulation in Adobe Photoshop.

Project 1 **Ship's wheel decoration**

Between the saloon/galley and the sleeping area is a large hatch that can be removed to let more light into the sleeping area, or if you just want to open up a bit to gain more space and to socialise. We thought the hatch was the perfect place for a wall decoration so, having painted the hatch white, we cut a ship's wheel out of self-adhesive brushed aluminium vinyl. The frame on the hatch made it look almost picture-like – but nicer!

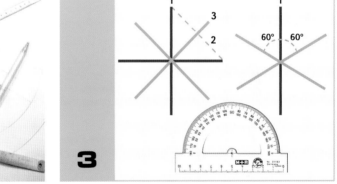

▲ Start off by painting the base. We painted the hatch white. Paint as many coats as necessary, letting each one dry for the stated time.

▲ For the decoration itself, you will need:
- Self-adhesive brushed aluminium vinyl, or whatever look you fancy. It is available from most art shops or car decoration companies.
- Ruler – preferably steel, if you have one.
- Snap-blade knife or scalpel with a curved blade. This makes it easier to cut out the round shapes.
- Large calliper, or a reliable tape measure with an ordinary flat drawing pin.
- Ballpoint pen – pencil does not stay on as well.

To make the ship's wheel: Draw on the back of the vinyl. Do not press too hard with the pen in case you make a mistake, as the marks will show on the front, especially if the surface is glossy.

▲ There are ship's wheels with six spokes and ones with eight handles. If you want to make a steering wheel with six spokes (less fiddly), similar to the one I made, the easiest thing is to use a protractor.

Now all you have to do is draw the steering wheel the way you want it. Decide on the width of the spokes, size of the hub, breadth of the outer ring and what shape you want the handles to be. I chose slightly oval for the end knobs, but if you want a sleeker look you can skip the knobs and draw curved, tapered handles instead.

4

▲ To make a circle without a calliper, push a drawing pin right through the tape measure at the desired measurement (half the diameter of the circle, plus 1 cm/0.4 in).

5

▲ Keep the drawing pin pressed against the centre of the ship's wheel. Put the pen through the outer hole in the tape measure and move it round in a circle.

6

▲ Cut out your ship's wheel. If you care about the surface beneath, remember to put something protective between it and the ship's wheel.

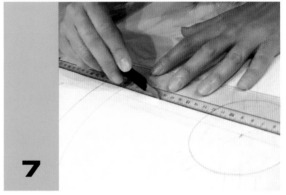

7

▲ Cut out the straight lines against a ruler. If you use a plastic ruler, angle the knife so you do not cut into the ruler.

8

▲ To avoid unevenness and folds when you put up your ship's wheel, use application tape or water and detergent. The soapy water prevents the vinyl from sticking immediately, allowing a couple of minutes to adjust the positioning of your decoration. Ready!

Project 2 **Personalised fo'c'sle door**

In the very middle of the boat, where the boat's two fixed berths are, we wanted to make it a bit cosy. We settled on new covers for the cushions (made of mould-resistant, dirt- and water-repellent Tempotest fabric from Italian manufacturer Para), and curtains for the compartments along the sides, to stop things from falling out, but also because it looks neat and attractive. New comfortable mattresses meant we had to raise the frame. Instead of trying to match the wood to the existing finish, we painted the new edge white, which would match the rest of the new interior.

We also found a great place to decorate – the fo'c'sle door. The signal flag 'M' went perfectly with the compartment curtains.

1

▲ If the motif has straight lines, it is easy to mock it up in sticky tape first, to get a proper idea of size and position.

2

▲ Next measure it, to ensure it is symmetrical. Leave the tape on to use as a template when you paint on the base colour.

3

▲ We wanted a slightly worn, 'distressed' look, so first we used a lighter blue, as a primer.

4

▲ Then we painted a coat of darker blue over the whole door, painted the cross white, and finally scratched a little here and there, for that distressed look. We were happy with the result!

Project 3 Red carpet treatment

Floor areas on boats are rarely symmetrical with straight lines, and are therefore difficult to measure. If there is already a carpet to be replaced, it is a piece of cake – all you need do is take the carpet home and use it as a template. We didn't have a carpet, so the only thing to do was to cut out a template in the boat. Start by cutting out roughly the size you need, with a good margin, so you do not have to lug a whole roll or fit too much paper into a tight space.

We chose a pale carpet so that the passage wouldn't feel too dark. We would just have to remember to keep dirty, wet shoes off it!

1

▲ If you have a mast post that goes through the floor, start by measuring and cutting out a hole for it.

2

▲ Cut the hole as precisely as possible, so the paper will not slide. It is good to reinforce it with some tape. A cut is needed to get the paper round the mast.

3

▲ Press the paper outwards against the edges of the floor, and mark with a blunt pencil or similar. Make the edges even – it is helpful to use a ruler along the straight parts. Then cut away the surplus.

4

▲ The template is ready!

5

▲ Place the upside-down template on the upside-down carpet and mark with a suitable pen. Put some weights on the template to keep it in place (see page 36 for more tips).

6

▲ Remove the template and cut. Put a thin board or similar underneath the carpet as protection.

7

▲ We were a little bit nervous when we put the carpet in place, but it fitted perfectly.

Our new-look fo'c'sle, complete with carpet and decorated door.

This is not Roobarb, but a 1970s Hallberg-Rassy 35 Rasmus with original mahogany interior.

02

THE CABIN

>> 'REAL' TEAK FLOOR IN THE CABIN

The 26-year-old, tired plywood floor on board *Roobarb* was badly worn and damaged from dropped tools, and it had dark damp patches. The veneer on a plywood board is often thinner than 1 mm (0.04 in), and sanding it down is difficult. Instead I chose to make a grooved floor with teak veneer and real deck-caulking compound on top of the old board. The result was better than expected.

I wanted to create a traditional look for the new floor, so I bought 2.8-mm (0.11-in) thick teak veneer, which I attached with epoxy glue onto the old floor plate. The veneer was then left to set for 24 hours while the epoxy hardened.

When it had hardened, I used a hand-held surface-milling cutter and cut 6-mm (0.24-in) wide grooves, not quite as deep as the thickness of the veneer (approx. 2 mm/0.08 in deep). As the veneer was 200 mm (8 in) wide, I divided it into equal widths (approx. 55 mm/2 in), like 'planks'.

The veneer had quite uneven edges and we evened out some areas with a carpet knife. But since we had chosen to make a groove just over the joint, many flaws were perfectly covered and we avoided the somewhat tricky task of trying to cut or saw the edges of the rather thick veneer, to make them even.

DIFFICULT CARTRIDGE GUN
It took a lot of effort to make the caulking compound in the grooves even – using a cheap cartridge gun did not make it a particularly easy job so select a good quality power-gun.

This is how good the result can be if you spend a few hours making your own floorboards, to replace the old, worn plywood floor.

PROJECT LOG

TIME: approx. 8 hours.

COST: approx. £125 – veneer about £60, epoxy kit £50 (enough for more projects), deck-caulking compound about £15, for a floor area just over 1.2 m² (133 sq ft).

SKILL LEVEL: easy.

TOOLS: hand-held surface-milling cutter if you choose veneer; a good cartridge gun makes the job easier; a sharp mortise chisel; oscillating sanding machine.

ENVIRONMENT: epoxy is strong glue and contact with skin should be avoided. Latex gloves are recommended to avoid getting epoxy glue and caulking compound on your hands.

Remember!

Deck caulking compound is extremely sticky to work with:

Protect work surfaces and yourself. Rubber gloves are a great help here, too! Special cleaning agents, such as Sika Hand Cleaner, are available, but only work on unhardened caulking compound.

Veneer easily becomes distorted when it dries. Use weights when gluing.

If you have the veneer convex side up, it is easier to press it down when gluing. However, still remember not to press the veneer too hard, so that all the epoxy is squeezed out; it works best when it is in an even layer, about 1 mm (0.04 in) thick between the surfaces to be stuck together.

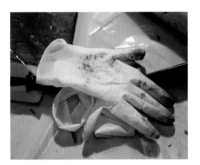

Latex gloves are very practical to avoid getting epoxy glue and caulking compound on your hands.

ALTERNATIVES TO VENEER

We looked into several alternatives to the rather arduous method of laying veneer. There is something called decking plywood, with both white and black 'grooves' of other wood types. The thickness ranges from 6 mm (0.24 in), which can be glued to the old boat floor, up to 22 mm (0.9 in), if you want a completely new floor.

Another option we considered was using teak planks. With a 6 mm (0.24 in) thickness and 44–50 mm (1.7–2 in) width, boards can be easier to lay than veneer. Either you lay them edge to edge and then cut the grooves, or you can use a pallet-deck spacer between each board. It is best to screw the boards down to secure them during the gluing process.

Decking plywood with 'real' rubber caulked grooves can be ordered from joinery mills or imported from Asia from various websites. However, it is almost three times as expensive to order this from a carpenter as it is to use the types we suggest.

Material	Thickness	Approx. cost/m²
Plywood flooring	6–22 mm (0.24–0.9 in)	£78 (13 mm/0.5 in)
Teak planks	from 6 mm (0.24 in)	£81 (6 mm/0.24 in)
Veneer	0.8–2.8 mm (0.03–0.11 in)	£73 (2.8 mm/0.11 in)
Decking plywood (with rubber-caulked grooves)	13–18 mm (0.5–0.7 in)	£214 (13 mm/0.5 in)

I used an ordinary wooden spatula to spread the caulking compound, and thus managed to get a pretty even result. With a better cartridge gun, I could possibly have avoided this extra effort. There are battery powered guns that give a very neat result.

We also had some problems with the veneer; due to the pieces we had cut to measure towards the end of the project, we had not been consistent with which side faced up. Since the veneer was slightly warped, the pieces did not quite fit.

However, most things were sorted out with the sanding machine afterwards.

If I were to do this again, I think I would opt for 6-mm (0.24-in) teak boards; it would probably have made it easier to glue to the base. And it is possible that the result would have looked even better.

A hand-held surface-milling cutter is good for making grooves easily. Teak is very hard, which means the material grinds heavily on the cutting steel. Quality pays, at least if you have a lot of grooves to make.

1

▲ The base is sanded to an even surface. Badly damaged spots may need repair putty applying, but we are relying on the epoxy glue to fill the minor defects.

2

▲ The engine room insulation mass on one of the three floorboards was also removed.

3

▲ We are planning how to lay the veneer pieces, to have as little surplus material as possible. There was still the odd spot that needed to have to pieces joined.

4

▲ The wooden surfaces that are to be glued with epoxy are first de-greased with acetone, since teak is an oily wood type.

5

▲ The epoxy glue is made up and both surfaces are prepared with thickened epoxy first, in order to make the binding effect really strong.

6

▲ The remaining epoxy is mixed with filler, which makes very effective glue; the texture should be thick like ketchup.

7

▲ Lots of cardboard boxes filled with heavy magazines compress the veneer and the plywood board overnight.

8

▲ The grooves are cut with a hand-held surface-milling cutter, guided by a long ruler secured with clamps. The grooves are only cut to a 2-mm (0.08-in) depth.

9

▲ To make a uniform pattern, the veneer was glued to all three floorboards at the same time, then sawn apart with a Fein saw (or use a thin Japanese saw).

10

▲ All edges next to the grooves were masked with tape to avoid most of the mess from the caulking compound.

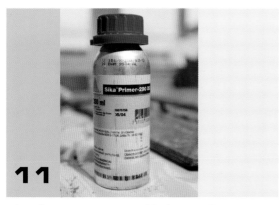

11

▲ All grooves were primed for better adhesion. But the caulked base was not taped, as you would on teak decking, because the floor is inside and therefore protected from the elements.

12

▲ A cartridge gun was used to inject the caulking compound slowly and systematically, to fill the grooves from the bottom up.

13

▲ Make sure all the grooves are filled slightly to excess – a concave spatula can be used to distribute the compound more evenly.

14

▲ The tape is removed after the compound has hardened for a while. If you wait too long it is difficult to get it off.

15

▲ When the caulking compound has been left to harden for a couple of days the only thing left to do is to sand the whole surface with 120-grade sandpaper. Done!

>> RAG RUGS IN A BOAT?

Many boatowners feel that traditional rag rugs are not the best choice for a boat. Possibly true, but a rug in a boat can be quite practical, because it collects dirt. What should you look for in carpets or rugs for the boat?

First of all, let's get something straight – even rag rugs can be suitable to use on board and give a certain cosy feeling.

But carpets or mats made of a synthetic material are far better to use on board. Most types of carpets can be cut to size for the boat floor.

The disadvantage with carpet on the floor is that when the boat is rolling, the foothold suffers. There are special anti-slip carpets or you can put non-slip netting under the carpet. Unfortunately, anti-slip carpets may leave an ugly residue on the plywood board. Another option is to use Velcro tape or press studs to keep the carpet in place.

TIPS FROM THE PROFESSIONALS

Carpet expert Stefan Palmkvist maintains that the most important features for an onboard carpet are that the material is synthetic and that the backing does not dry out and peel. He also suggests to go for a darker colour, because pale colours easily become soiled after a few years in the boat. On the subject of colours, in Stefan's opinion boat owners are very conventional and tend to stick with blue, beige or grey carpets.

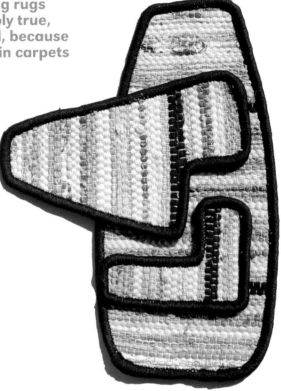

'Things have progressed since the 1970s, especially when it comes to materials. Fortunately the popular colours yellow, orange and brown have almost disappeared altogether,' says Stefan. 'But they will probably come back.'

The easiest way when ordering carpets is to use the old carpets or mats from the boat, or make cardboard templates. Do not use newspaper or plastic sheeting. Take into account that good templates for a whole boat take at least half a day, if not a day, to make. The templates should be exactly the size you want them; the edge-stitching does not add to the width.

MAINTENANCE

Carpet maintenance is easy – remove the carpets from the boat in the winter and store them in a dry, well-ventilated place, preferably laid out. If they are rolled up, the pile should face outwards.

Cost

Buying remnants can be one way of keeping the cost down. Estimate around £30–35 per m². If a carpet is ordered, it can cost £50–100 per m², or even more.

The price per m² is based on the gross surface area, which means you pay for what is cut away as well. If you have your own carpet that you want edge-stitched, it costs about £7 per metre.

Boats often require specially measured carpets that can fit around bulkheads and table legs.

Most carpets can easily be cleaned, either with a rented carpet cleaner or by scrubbing the carpet by hand with a brush, using soft soap or an eco-friendly detergent and warm water, in the marina or at home in the garage.

Hang the carpet and rinse it, and the dirt will come off in the process. If it is a smaller mat, it can be cleaned in a heavy-duty washing machine.

Many carpets can even be cleaned with a high-pressure jet.

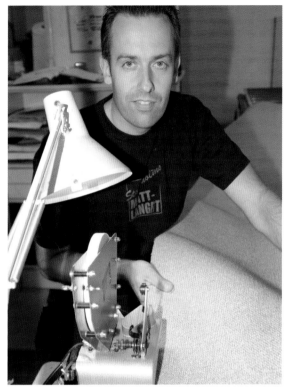

Stefan at the blanket-stitching machine.

A white carpet looks good in a photograph, but is not very practical in the long run. But it was lovely to walk on.

*Right: Jenni makes templates out of brown paper on board **Roobarb**. A carpet remnant does not cost much.*

>> NEW CUSHIONS – A FACELIFT FOR THE BOAT

New cushion covers are a relatively easy way to give the cabin a completely new 'feel'. Boat-cover maker Elin Wanselius shows us both how the professionals work and a fairly simple way of making your own fresh new cushions.

Buying new cushions often costs several hundred pounds if you go to a boat-cover maker. For a 9-m (30-ft) boat, it will cost from about £1000, depending on the price of the fabric you choose.

An important start to making cushions that fit is always to make good templates (more about this in the next section).

Always take the measurements straight from the boat, rather than the old cushions. Old foam shrinks and changes shape.

Use a carpenter's rule to measure the height from the bottom of the cushion to the top edge and jot it down in centimetres or inches onto the template plastic. If it is a complicated shape, measure in 10-cm

(4-in) increments and add a plus or minus sign before the measurement to indicate how much it needs to be chamfered, and in which direction; if it is quite simple, then every 50 cm (20 in) is enough.

SIMPLIFY

Consider sending the complicated cushions off to a professional. Or simplify the shape – you will probably get an acceptable result, even if the cushion does not sit 100% against the hull, or whatever creates the surface angle.

Cutting foam plastic is not an easy task. A new, sharp snap-blade knife works quite well; an electric bread-knife is even better.

Elin Wanselius at Cover Up busy at her sewing machine, showing us how she works when she makes boat pads and cushions.

ZIPS AND WADDING

Fitting a zip can make it easier to wash the cover when it is dirty, but often it is just as easy to unstitch and re-stitch the short side. If you are making a long pad for a berth, you could leave a slot of 60–70 cm (24–28 in) open on the long side of the cover to squeeze the pad through. Then you can stitch it up by hand.

Adding wadding to the pad makes it a bit softer, and also fills the cover better and makes any little flaws less visible.

Covered buttons ensure the pad and the cover stay together without sliding; but if it is a sleeping pad, on the other hand, buttons are not that comfortable to sleep on.

ELIN'S TIPS

■ **There are some providers of professional boat-covers and accessories, such as sailrite.com, who will sell directly to consumers.**

■ **There are some providers of professional boat-covers and accessories who will sell directly to consumers, but they can be expensive. Jersey fabric, wadding, pressed fabrics and sometimes synthetic cushion fabrics are also available at a slightly lower cost from some cut-price textile suppliers.**

■ **The stockinet under-cover easily snags in the zip – pull carefully.**

■ **You can make your own covered buttons, but it does not cost very much to get help from the professionals (about £2 per button). Make sure the buttons are rustproof.**

PRACTISE FIRST

If you have not done very much sewing before – and boat cushions are one of those projects that boat owners tend to attempt with little experience or knowledge – I recommend you start by making a smaller 'test pad' first, perhaps from remnants, to learn how best to do the various steps.

And then it is like so many other things – measure twice, cut once...

Professionals use a special keyhole saw to cut foam. You will find other, easier DIY techniques in Chapter 7.

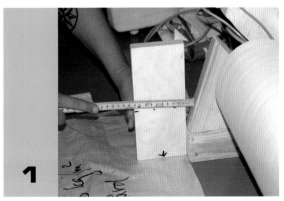

1

▲ Elin shows how she works with a carpenter's rule and a piece of wood, where the cushion height is marked to get the measure for possible bevelling.

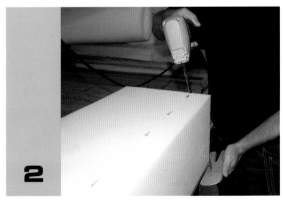

2

▲ You can let a specialist cut the foam with a band saw, or in this case, a special keyhole saw with cross-cutting blades is being used to chamfer the foam for Elin.

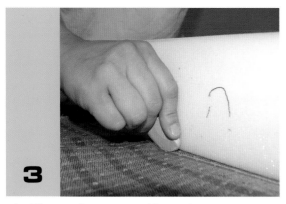

3

▲ Elin uses the cut-out cushion as the pattern to outline and cut out the top and side pieces, with a seam allowance of about 0.5 cm (0.2 in).

4

▲ Using an overlock sewing machine, she overlocks the raw edges of the fabric after cutting out the pieces, so they do not fray.

5

▲ Having cut and stitched the side section to the right length, Elin stitches it to the top piece, with both pieces inside out.

6

▲ Sew a second seam a few millimetres from the outer edge to get a better fit and, more importantly, to reinforce the seam.

7

▲ Use a piece of cheap felt for the underside of the cushion, cut to the same size as the cushion, plus 1 cm (0.4 in) for the seam. Stitch it to the side, as with the top piece.

8

▲ If you choose to add a zip, stitch it to the bottom piece and then cut it open. Felt does not fray and no edging is needed.

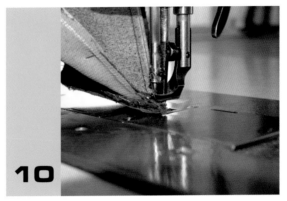

▲ The seams of the bottom piece are snipped at the corners so they will not ruck up.

▲ The corners are tricky, so take care. It takes longer to undo mistakes than getting it right from the start.

▲ The corners are inclined to ruck up when the cover is turned the right way out so smooth them out.

▲ The topside of the foam is covered with wadding to make the pad more 'cushion-like' and to fill the cover more easily.

▲ Spray glue is applied to ensure the wadding does not slip on the foam.

▲ The wadding is cut round the corners and the edges are spray-glued in place.

15 ▲ The whole thing is then eased into a stockinet cover, which makes it easier to get the pad in and out of the fabric cover. The stockinet can be stitched round the edges.

16 ▲ Getting the pad into the fabric cover is akin to wrestling, and Elin considers this to be one of the trickiest parts of the process.

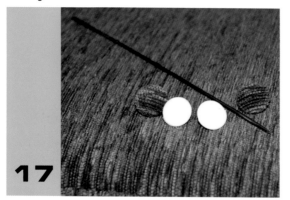

17 ▲ Buttons are used to secure the fabric to the pad. Insert the needle vertically and fasten the covered button to a cheaper button on the underside of the cushion.

A SIMPLER VERSION

Our boat-cover maker Elin shows how to make your own attractive cushions using a slightly simplified technique, where instead of stitching several pieces of fabric together, you 'tuck and pinch' the corners of one piece to make a box shape. According to Elin, even boat owners who are not used to sewing can make really good cushions using this method. However, bear in mind that this technique is best for square or rectangular cushions, which have no complicated chamfering.

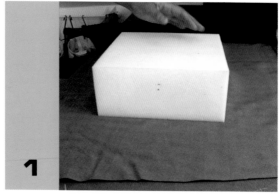

1 ▲ Use the cut-out pad as a template. Position the pad with enough fabric around it to cover the top and sides in one piece, including a seam allowance.

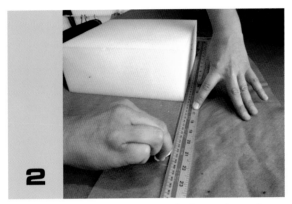

2 ▲ Using a wax pencil and metal rule, mark out the shape of the pad on the back of the fabric.

3 ▲ Extend the shape to include the sides of the pad.

4 ▲ The finished shape will be a stubby cross.

5 ▲ Cut out the fabric, allowing an extra 0.5 cm (0.2 in) for the seams. Overlock the edges of the fabric to prevent fraying.

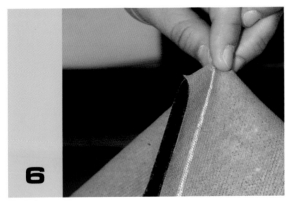

6 ▲ Pinch the corners just above the drawn lines, then stitch the seams. This is the trickiest step. Do it carefully to get a neat result.

7 ▲ The finished article looks like a box. Test to see if the pad fits.

▲ Use cheap felt for the bottom, cut to the same size as the pad, plus 1 cm (0.4 in) for the seam.

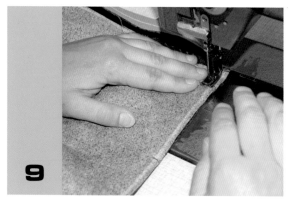

▲ Stitch the bottom to the completed 'box' along three sides. The fourth side is left open to insert the foam pad.

▲ Tuck in and pin the fourth short side.

▲ Now the fourth side can be stitched by hand, using a double thickness of thread.

▲ Ready! This method is simpler than the professional method, and may be more suitable for the first of your own projects.

>> A SEWING MACHINE FIT FOR THE JOB

Sewing through thick fabrics or several layers may prove a tough job for a domestic sewing machine, and very few people have access to an industrial sewing machine.

Björn Åqvist has been mending sails and making boat covers since the 1970s. Here he shares some insight into what to expect from sewing machines.

Perhaps you already have a sewing machine at home, or one you can borrow from a relative or friend. Sewing machines are durable, and it is not uncommon to find homes that still have a 1960s sewing machine tucked away in a cupboard. If not, a quick search of the advertising websites will normally come up with almost anything you ask for, from industrial machines to the old Husqvarna that granny used.

SEWING MACHINE BASICS

If you have an older machine, it may be worthwhile giving it a clean around the moving parts (with a vacuum cleaner and a small brush used to clean an electric razor, for example), and oil it well with sewing machine oil. Using sharp, new needles, practise on pieces of scrap cloth if you are not used to the sewing machine. Older machines can be sent out for service, and, once in good working order, many older models can handle heavier jobs than one might think.

FEATURES

Björn, whose job is to repair sails, compared three heavy-duty sewing machines that were tested on several layers of boat-cover canvas and sailcloth. He was surprised that even the older machines managed several layers.

BJÖRN'S 5 BEST TIPS

1. Test the machine to make sure it can handle the thickness of the layers of material you intend to sew.

2. Measure *twice*, then cut and sew.

3. Check out the work of the professionals and copy them.

4. Clearly defined edge markings, sewing lines and cross marks make the job easier.

5. Experiment and don't lose heart if it is not perfect the first time.

Björn's general impression was that the old, green Husqvarna type 20 could handle the thick cloth just as well as the newer 2000 model.

Janome Easy Jeans, a lightweight model of sewing machine, is not that far from Björn's own industrial machines, and could be classed as semi-professional, according to Björn.

THE FIRST PROJECT

What I have noticed among boat owners is that many actually use a sewing machine for the first time when they are going to sew something for the boat. Using a sewing machine is not particularly difficult, but we were all beginners once.

Also, a large number of men are to be found behind the sewing machine when it comes to sewing projects for boats – even though they would never normally dream of mending clothes, they are happy to tackle sewing new cushion covers for the whole boat. I know, because I am one of them!

My first project (as an adult) was precisely that – making new pads for the berths. The last time I had used a sewing machine was in textile handicrafts at secondary school in the 1980s.

The best thing to do is to take a few remnants of cover canvas (or the type of cloth you intend to use) and test different kinds of stitching, how much the cloth pulls, and perhaps sew a zip, if you plan to use those.

Above are some of Björn's tips on what techniques and aids can be used for sewing seams, and inserting windows and zips in boat cover canvas.

Sewing thread

Industry standard thread is manufactured by, among others, Hemingway & Bartlett and Bainbridge, part of the Dabond trademark. A V92 spool costs about £75.

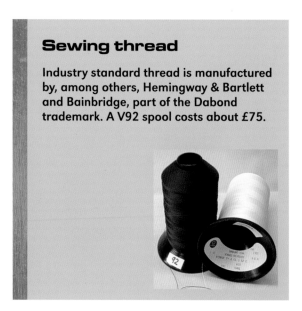

FOCUS   SEWING MACHINES

The classic green Husqvarna, model 20, was launched as early as 1953 and around 250,000 of this model were manufactured. It is easy to find a second-hand one for around £30.

Another very common sewing machine in our homes is the Husqvarna 2000, launched in 1966. Over one million machines were made. Available second-hand for around £100.

A modern semi-professional machine, the Janome Easy Jeans (Elna 3210, Bernina 1008 and Pfaff 1529 have similar features; the latter two cost a little more) has a strong motor and can sew through several layers of thick canvas and sailcloth. It has an extra high presser foot lift. Add a presser foot with Teflon coating or a roller. Costs about £500 new.

In the US, Sailrite manufacture sail seam machines, which have a huge following, with a 3.2-kg (7-lb) flywheel (optional extra) that makes it easy to help to pull manually when it sticks. It can do stitches up to 6 mm (0.24 in) long, 5 mm (0.2 in) when zigzagging. And it handles several layers of sailcloth.

Nowadays it can be bought in Europe, and costs around £800; the flywheel is another £100.

Left: An industrial sewing machine with zigzag feature can sometimes be bought second-hand. The Pfaff 138 has been the sailmaker's favourite for decades. The motor is located under the table, which is included. Costs from £400 second-hand.

NEEDLE, THREAD AND AIDS

Björn used a so-called 'jeans needle', size 90, for all three machines. The thread is synthetic/cotton No. 40. The advantage is that the cotton coating swells when it rains, and seals the seams a little more.

Experience has shown that for difficult projects it is best to change to a 100% synthetic thread, which is smoother than the cotton mix. Björn also used a Teflon-coated presser foot, and applied clear Teflon spray to the canvas when the machines started to labour.

The machines were set at a fairly long stitch length and normal thread tension. Björn's advice is to experiment with threads and stitches.

CLOTH AND CANVAS

Common brands of canvas for boat covers and sprayhoods are Sunbrella and Markilux 37. Björn used these when testing the sewing machines.

These products are available both uncoated and coated. The coating on the back of the canvas makes it waterproof for the first few years, after which it is time to re-impregnate it. These two manufacturers have a large market share and are commonly used by boat-cover makers.

The domestic machines were better at handling the uncoated types of canvas.

Björn wanted to test the limit for domestic machines. Some of the tests were too much for the older machines; the modern machine, however, could handle all types of cloth, even though it was slower than an industrial machine. But Björn considers this a possible advantage, since it is easier to keep up when the machine does not go too fast, if you are not used to sewing machines.

SEWING

Pin, or mark how the cloths are going to fit together with edge and cross marks, and possibly also a sewing line to sew along. Ordinary pins are too weak. Upholstery pins or moulding pins No. 2 will work.

'Do not try to help the machine along by pulling at the cloth,' Björn advises, 'because the needle easily ends up on the presser foot and breaks, and the needle bar and clip are displaced. Try different settings, needles and threads. Sometimes a thinner thread helps, in which case just sew an extra seam.'

FOCUS

Not all textiles are suitable on board. Damp and sunlight soon devour some, while others fare better. Here is a brief overview of what to consider when buying textiles for the boat.

NATURAL OR SYNTHETIC

Cotton is among the cheapest and easiest fabrics available for sewing. Unfortunately, cottons do not tend to withstand the onboard environment of damp and UV-light.

Synthetic fabrics are actually better suited – they can withstand the environment much better and thus last considerably longer than natural fabrics.

One way of testing whether a fabric is synthetic or cotton is to set fire to a small piece. If it burns with a thick black smoke, it is synthetic. If, however, it does not burn easily and mostly carbonises when you hold a lighter to the edge, it is probably cotton. Impregnated cotton can burn very well, though, so this is a rule of thumb with some exceptions.

CUSHION FABRIC

The cushion fabric on board should also be synthetic. However, I do think it is a good idea to make protective covers from cheaper (cotton) fabric, to keep the original covers clean. This will usually cost less than a strong cushion fabric.

You will also have the original covers, still looking fresh and new, if the day comes when you want to sell the boat.

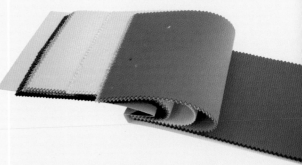

Choose your fabrics for the boat carefully – good quality pays in the long run.

FABRIC FACTS

CANVAS AND BOAT-COVER CLOTH

You can cover cushions and mattresses in canvas or boat-cover cloth made of acrylic, which is hardwearing but, because it is impregnated, not so comfortable to lie on. It is normally coated with Teflon (the trademark for fluorocarbon) or polyurethane. Plain boat-cover cloth comes in around 20 colour combinations. There are some patterns available, but unfortunately these are not common.

Acrylic, which is the most common material, cannot withstand high temperatures and should be washed at maximum 40°C/104°F, or by hand with soap solution and a soft brush. It can also be sent off for professional cleaning.

For outdoor use, only a 100% acrylic cloth should be considered.

PVC-COATED CLOTH

A PVC-coated cloth (originally made under the trade-mark 'Galon') is durable and good for cushions and seats in the cockpit, where they are exposed to rain.

Samples of sun-, mould- and water-resistant Tempotest fabrics, from the Italian company Para. 'Fig Leaves' (right) now features in three colour combinations on board Roobarb.

FABRIC TIPS

■ Make sure the fabric is not too stretchy, as it can wrinkle. Cushions covered in this kind of fabric can look as if they are sagging.

■ A bold pattern does not look soiled as quickly as light or plain colours.

■ Avoid check or striped fabrics, which make it hard to get a good fit. And boat cushions are seldom straight shapes, so checks and stripes are difficult to work with.

■ Navy cushion fabric is the most popular choice; dark green and red are more unusual. Then come the other colours – brown and orange are slowly making a comeback, having been very common in the 1970s.

■ Read the laundry labels and ask how much the fabric will shrink – otherwise it may be difficult to get the foam pad back into the cover after washing.

■ If the boat has old cushions that you would like to revive, bear in mind that foam ages quickly. If your budget allows for it, buy new foam – do not just change the old cushion covers.

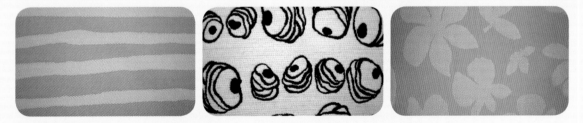

Below: Colour samples of PVC-coated cloth.

03
THE BERTHS

>> SLEEP LIKE A BABY

Why should you not sleep as well in the boat as at home, and especially if you spend several weeks every summer on board? Making a mattress for the berth is not much more difficult than making your own cushions – but the resulting comfort is considerable.

Those of us who are getting on a bit may suffer from backache a few days into the boating holiday. Old, sagging mattresses in the berths may be one reason. It is not unusual for the foam rubber mattresses on board to be 20, even 30 years old (like they were on the project boat *Roobarb!*). Foam rubber breaks down with time; it loses its springiness and becomes flat and hard to lie on. Simply making new textile covers for the old foam rubber mattresses is false economy.

MAKE YOUR OWN
Sprung mattresses are still fairly uncommon in leisure boats, since they are more expensive than ordinary pads to order to size. But if you suffer with a bad back, or if you plan to spend long periods on board, like I do, then it may be worth the extra expense. If you make them yourself from a kit, it does not really take that long.

The most difficult part of the whole project was to make the cover fit. Sewing on a good machine is not that hard, but to unstitch what has just been sewn is hard labour. Heeding the saying, 'measure twice, cut once' is an absolute must if you are a beginner at this – especially as good-quality boat cushion cloth costs over £30–40 per metre.

I have made several different cushions in order to find the best method.

THE FIRST STEPS
When I set out to make my own sprung mattress, I started by visiting a company where they manufacture beds and sprung mattresses for boats. There I was able to see how the professionals

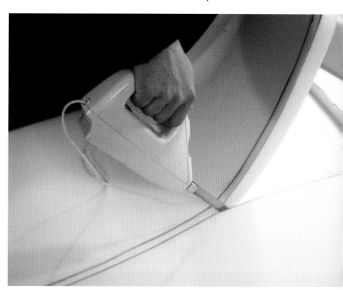

Using an old electric bread-knife, foam rubber is cut into shapes that together will make a comfortable sprung mattress.

construct a made-to-order bed in a few minutes, and gained an insight into how to make a sprung mattress. The principle is quite simple – you build a box of foam rubber, add some springs, put on the lid and insert it into a fabric cover. The visit boosted my confidence in making a mattress and now I was sure I could handle the project.

I also took the opportunity of buying some ready-cut foam rubber pieces from the company, as a kind of building kit.

Different levels of firmness and materials in the pads give the mattresses different characteristics. Read more about foam rubber in Chapter 7.

MATERIALS

Apart from the foam rubber from the mattress company, I needed quite a few accessories. Collecting all the different pieces from all over town took some time, and if you live in a village or small town this may be one of the steps that requires most time and money. Fortunately, it is becoming easier to order things off the internet and have them delivered.

I bought the synthetic cloth for the cover from a hypermarket that sells offcuts and remnants. While I was there I also bought some felt, which does not attract mould as easily, to use as the bottom cover; a 2-m (79-in) zip; a berth-length of wadding (just over 3 cm/1 in thick); and a stockinet cover that keeps the mattress and the wadding together when you insert them into the cover.

The navy cloth was quite boring and conventional, and it was the last piece they had and not big enough for both berths. So I later purchased a new fabric, to brighten up the cabin and make it more attractive.

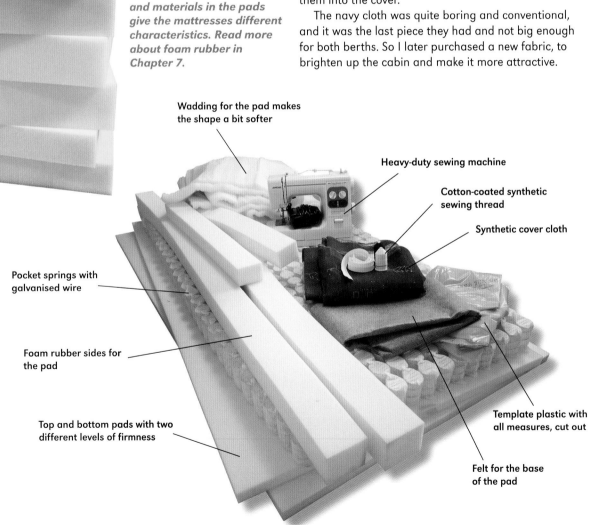

Wadding for the pad makes the shape a bit softer

Heavy-duty sewing machine

Cotton-coated synthetic sewing thread

Synthetic cover cloth

Pocket springs with galvanised wire

Foam rubber sides for the pad

Top and bottom pads with two different levels of firmness

Template plastic with all measures, cut out

Felt for the base of the pad

In the past, I have chosen a traditional fabric for the pad and made a loose cover with a bright cotton fabric, thinking that it could always be replaced after a few years, when it became worn and not so attractive. The fresh, conventional fabric is still underneath, which helps to sell the boat eventually.

The new covers were made in a white fabric with a special silicon coating for better resistance to sunlight and dirt. That part of the project was covered in Chapter 1.

I found thread for the sewing machine at a boat-cover company, but fabric stores also sell a brand you can use on smaller spools.

There are several types of spray glue on the market. Foam rubber is difficult to glue and requires special contact adhesive, which is simplest to use from a spray can.

SPRINGS

I also did some research to find out what steel springs I could use. Most springs for ordinary beds and indoor use are made of untreated steel and could rust in the damp atmosphere on board if not treated by, for example, spray-coating them first. However, I found the Swedish company Stjernfjädrar, a large manufacturer of springs for ordinary pocket-sprung beds. They make a pocket spring core that is coated with zinc and thus rustproof, which is perfect for the boat.

Pocket-sprung cores have steel springs, each glued into a fabric pouch. Each coil can spring without impact on the adjacent one, which allows the mattress to adapt extremely well to the body's shape in different sleeping positions.

The pocket springs are 9 cm (3.5 in) high and ideal for a berth where all you do is sleep. However, they are not as suitable for seat pads, since it is easy for one's behind to 'sink through'. Foam rubber is better for the saloon, but then they are not as comfortable to sleep on.

The metal springs come with different levels of resistance, depending on the gauge of the wire in the coil. Around 1.5–2 mm (0.06–0.08 in) are the most common gauges, and for zinc-coated springs 'medium resistance' is about 1.75 mm (0.07 in).

BUILD A BOX

With the material from the mattress company, I was able to start building. I bought ready-cut foam rubber that fitted an ordinary 105-cm (3 ft 6 in) wide sprung bed, i.e. as wide as the widest part of the berth at the head end. The rest was cut away with an electric

bread-knife to the template that I had measured out in the boat.

It is quite an easy process. You build a 'box' into which you place the cut pocket-sprung mattress. It was not difficult to cut the right dimensions and even though the material that surrounded the pocket springs was rather tough to cut through, it was done in under a half hour. The shape does end up stepped, however, since a berth is rarely straight. Where there are gaps, you just have to fill them with triangular shapes made out of the leftover foam rubber.

Then the pieces are glued together with spray contact adhesive. However, it was not that easy to find a spray glue (read more in Chapter 7). When you read the warning text on the back, it does not appear to be a health-friendly product to use in general. Good ventilation, a fume respirator mask and rubber gloves are a must.

Foam rubber is hard to glue, but spray glue does stick fairly well – just glue the pieces together and press as hard as you can, using a large wooden board to distribute the pressure.

A lot of glue is needed, and I had to go and buy more cans when the first ran out. It is good to have a few cans ready before starting the project.

PAD TWO

Initially, the idea was just to give the skipper's berth a pocket-sprung mattress.

The narrower berth on the port side already had a new mattress pad, made using a cheap 10-cm (4-in) foam mattress from Ikea and an ordinary bread-knife.

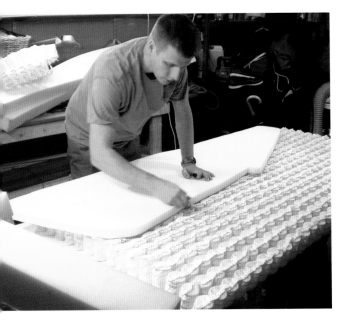

A mattress with pocket springs is so much more comfortable to sleep on than old, sagging foam. It is unexpectedly simple to make.

PROJECT LOG

SKILL LEVEL: medium.

TIME: approx. 2 hours + 4 hours for the cover.

TOOLS: heavy-duty sewing machine, sharp knives. Spray glue; several cans needed.

MATERIALS: foam plastic mattress material, consisting of several pieces that are joined to make a pad; 3 cm (1.2 in) top pad (28 kg/m³ soft) and 3 cm (1.2 in) bottom pad (28 kg/m³ firm).

Side strips approx. 10 x 9 cm (4 x 3.5 in) (35 kg/m³ firm). The bottom pad can be replaced by felt to reduce the total height by 3 cm (1.2 in).

But since the large pocket-sprung pad was cut diagonally, there were quite a lot of springs left over – enough to join them up for the other mattress pad as well. The spring pouches were not linked together, but the tests we had done suggested that this would not have any adverse effect on the functionality. Possibly the odd spring could be displaced or fold inside the mattress. That problem remains to be seen.

We also joined large panels of the leftover pieces of foam rubber for the new pad using spray glue. It holds it together very well – when everything is in the cover, the cloth also contributes to its strength.

Also, the second cushion had a more awkward shape with angled sides, which made the machine work hard, and I couldn't avoid the material puckering in places. Fortunately, it was on the underside of the cushion and thus not visible.

When I was cutting the double angles on the long side, I made a wrong cut because I misinterpreted the dimensions on the template I had made. I spray-glued the piece back on again, and it barely showed on the finished pad.

Had I cut the pad in situ on board, the problem would not have occurred. My advice is therefore to measure carefully, or do the trickiest cuts in situ, where you can check what you are doing against the berth's dimensions throughout.

SEWING

Since this was my very first attempt at sewing a pad, I started by test-sewing a short sample zip and also experimented with the corners. Despite not having much sewing experience, it was easier and more fun than I expected. But, of course, you make a few mistakes, and then you have to unstitch the work and sew it again.

There are various ways of sewing the covers for boat cushions and some of these can be found in Chapter 2 from page 38.

In conclusion, I can only say that nowadays I sleep better in the boat than I do in my old bed at home.

1

▲ Make a good template – the better the template, the simpler the job. There is more about making templates on pages 59–60.

▲ First, I draw the outline of the template(s) for the bottom and top foam rubber pieces, and make sure they are the right way round.

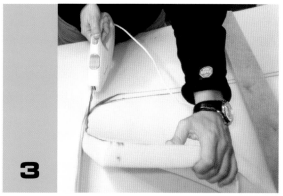

3

4

▲ An electric bread-knife cuts efficiently through the material. Be sure to keep the knife straight, as it is easy to end up with a wonky line.

▲ I also tried using a brand new and sharp snap-blade knife to cut the foam rubber. The result was not quite as good, but when the cover is on no one will notice an uneven edge.

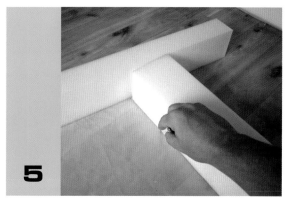

5

6

▲ I position the foam rubber pieces (10 cm/4 in wide) and then I can calculate the space in the centre that will remain for the pocket-sprung core.

▲ When the template is cut to the side dimensions, I can draw it onto the sprung base containing the springs in individual fabric pouches.

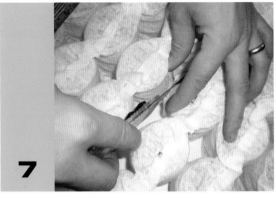

▲ Time to cut loose the pouches with the steel springs in a stepped shape, adapted to the shape of the pad. Cut on the correct side, so that the mattress only contains whole pouches.

7

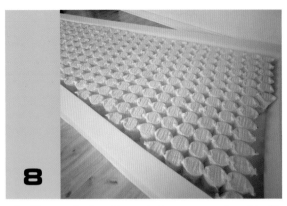

▲ The result when the pocket-sprung core is cut to fit.

8

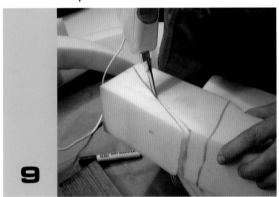

▲ The edges of foam rubber are cut to form the sides of the box that will contain the pocket springs.

9

▲ In the gaps that are formed, triangular pieces of foam rubber are cut out to fill the mattress properly.

10

▲ The fillers are cut to different shapes for different parts of the mattress.

11

▲ All the pieces are glued together with spray glue. The joints are pressed together with weighted boards while the contact adhesive dries.

12

13

▲ Spray glue is not healthy to inhale, so use a proper breathing mask with replacement filters, or work outdoors.

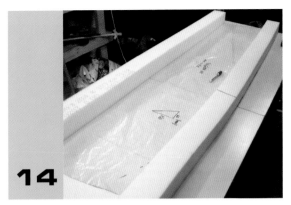

14

▲ The port-side berth is narrower and when we realised that there were enough leftover springs for the other mattress, we made a similar box...

15

▲ ...which was filled with a jigsaw of different-sized spring pieces. Although the pad is very narrow, you can lie comfortably on the pocket springs at full stretch.

16

▲ The electric bread-knife is used to trim whatever is needed. When the pad is covered, most of the unevenness disappears.

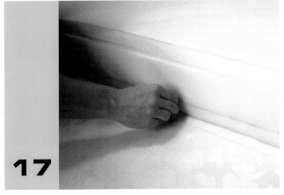

17

▲ The finished mattress is used as a template to cut the fabric for the cover.

18

▲ A cover is sewn using the method described earlier.

19

20

▲ A bit of wadding and a stockinet cover make the pad fluffier – and much harder to get into the cover. We cut open a bin-liner to make a temporary slippery cover, which made it easier.

▲ Having fitted and tested the mattresses in the boat for a few months now, I must say they are just as comfortable as a shop-bought mattress for home.

Talking to the professionals

Before I started making my own mattress pads, I visited a company that manufactures boat mattresses. They make thousands of beds and about a hundred boat mattresses per year.

Everywhere in the factory there are huge blocks of foam rubber, weighing close to 70 tonnes each. These are then cut down to the desired thickness with a band knife to make pads and mattresses.

Around 30 ordinary foam rubber mattresses for boats are made for every pocket-sprung mattress, according to an estimate from Jarmo Tolppanen, who works in the production of both ordinary sprung mattresses and boat mattresses at the factory.

Jarmo also says that it takes about an hour to cut the pieces and assemble a pocket-sprung mattress. Then Seija in the studio spends another hour or so sewing the cover. The price for a finished pocket-sprung mattresses is approximately £250 per m².

Huge blocks of foam rubber need to be cut down to the required size.

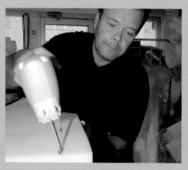

Jarmo chamfers the foam rubber with a special keyhole saw.

Seija sits at her machine and sews covers for both bed and boat mattresses. She says that navy is the most popular choice of fabric colour among boat owners.

>> MATTRESSES THAT MEASURE UP

Good templates are essential for the end result. Even if you leave the actual construction of the mattress pads to the professionals, you can make your own templates.

It is important that the template material is not too thin – choose a thick piece of plastic or board, so that it does not move. Fix it with tape in several places.

Spend time and effort on the template – the better it is, the easier it will be to make the pad.

1

▲ I start in the boat by measuring the berth with the aid of a piece of heavy plastic sheet, some tape, a felt-tip pen and sharp scissors.

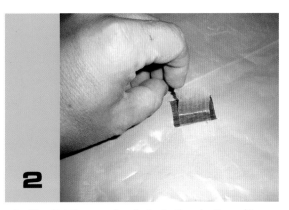

2

▲ Tip: Cut three or four holes in the plastic and tape over the hole to keep the plastic in place. That way the tape will not get in the way of the berth edges.

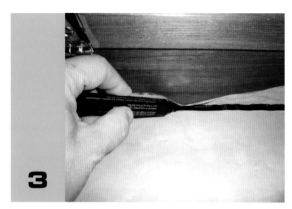

3

▲ Draw a line round the whole of the berth edge to get the base dimensions for the mattress.

4

▲ Cut out the template and double check the measurements while on the boat.

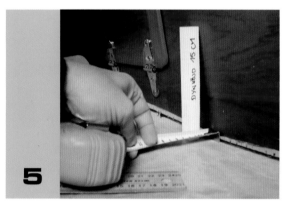

5

▲ If the edges of the pad are going to be chamfered, you can use a piece of wood or a set square the same height as the pad, to measure the chamfering with a carpenter's rule.

6

▲ A plus or minus sign before the measurement indicates how much it needs to be chamfered, and in which direction.

7

▲ Double chamfering is among the trickiest things to embark on. It is good to cut these angles in situ, to be sure you are cutting correctly.

8

▲ If you are happy with your old mattresses, you can use them as templates. But most old pads have, of course, lost their shape.

FOCUS HOW TO CUT FOAM RUBBER

The professionals use a type of keyhole saw with two blades cutting against each other. On a larger scale, they use a keyhole saw, or even a band knife (like a band saw but without teeth).

I bought a second-hand electric bread knife with two cross-cutting blades at an auction website for a fiver. These bread knives, popular in the 1980s, are still available to buy new, but can be hard to find. Ask around – maybe someone you know has one tucked away in the attic.

A cheap alternative is to use a new sharp snap-blade knife. The result will not be as neat, but when the pad is in the cover the slightly uneven surface does not show.

It works perfectly well to smooth uneven edges with a rotating bench grinder with coarse sandpaper, if you want a perfect surface.

My second-hand bread knife worked brilliantly. It came with two blades – the one with wave-shaped cutting teeth was much easier to work with, since it does not get stuck in the foam rubber.

There are short wave-shaped blades to buy for an ordinary keyhole saw. Unfortunately, they are usually too short to handle thick foam, so I have not tried these myself.

The professionals use a band saw or band knife, or a special keyhole saw fixed in a case, with a cutting blade in the centre. The case prevents the saw from getting stuck in the material.

04
THE GALLEY

>> IMPROVING THE GALLEY

The owners of this OE32, built in 1979, have carefully planned how every corner can be optimised. We took a look in their galley.

Since Lennart and Annchristin bought the boat *Shenandoah* ten years ago, they have rebuilt and adapted it to suit them. Lennart says he 'cannot let anything be just standard' and this has resulted in a series of clever solutions for the boat, in particular the galley.

Below: The galley has white laminate worktops, with a sink and cool box to the left and an LP-gas cooker on gimballed suspension in the centre. A strap around your hips leaves both hands free for cooking when the sea is rough. On the right are drawers with storage space behind. A compact but functional galley with lots of clever solutions.

Lennart and Annchristin spend all their summers on board their OE32 Shenandoah, and have made a considerable effort to get the boat exactly how they want it.

Above: A tray stored at the back of the cooker folds down as a worktop that follows the movements of the boat, since the cooker is on gimballed suspension. The spice rack is attached to a door that slides to one side to reveal storage behind.

Right, from top: The small wine glasses hang upside down in a sliding rack, so they won't fall off even in really rough weather.

In the cabinets behind the cooker is storage for things not often needed, tucked away beneath lids in the cabinet base.

Behind the cooker, compact jars allow the space to be used for storing items such as spaghetti. The thermos flasks, stored by the cooker, are filled with coffee in the morning and keep it hot almost the whole day.

Left: Above the galley – and elsewhere on the boat – a kerosene lamp has been placed in front of a brass-framed mirror, which reflects the light from the flame. A speaker on the bulkhead, clad in teak, provides music while you work.

Above: All the drawers have customised compartments to stop crockery knocking against each other. This drawer has two compartments, fitted precisely to accommodate cups and saucers.

Left: The inside of the door to the pots and pans cupboard is used to store cooking utensils.

Below left: On the opposite side of the galley is an extra work area, with a chopping board fitted into the top drawer by the navigation area.

Below: Plastic-coated brass bars keep the jars in place, and the knobs serve as hooks for tea towels.

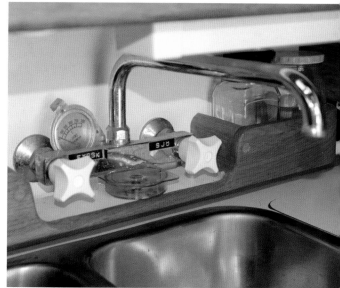

Above: The sinks have tray covers that hide the contents, or are used as an extra surface – usually for the dish draining rack, when the boat is moored.

Above right: From the cockpit, you step down onto the worktop. Storage jars fill the space behind the worktop and beneath the bridge deck.

Right: Both fresh and sea water intake is pressurised, regulated by ordinary kitchen taps.

Below: The space just below the sinks is often wasted. On Shenandoah, dishcloths, rubber gloves and scourers are stored here.

>> A FUNCTIONAL GALLEY

A convenient galley is an important part of a functional interior. More often than not, you have to accept the galley that comes with the boat – but if you are going to renovate and improve your boat anyway, why not take the opportunity to improve the areas that are not working well. Particularly in an older boat, where years of washing-up water have softened the worktop surfaces and old food remains lurk under the edge trim, it may well be worth considering starting from scratch.

Renovating the boat's galley is just the same as moving into a house or flat and ripping out the existing kitchen to install a brand new and fresh kitchen in the style you want.

Here are some ideas of what to consider if you want to change your galley.

WORKTOPS

Worktops in old boats have often had a pretty hard life – used both for preparing food and as an occasional workbench for repairs. The joints between the work surface and the edge in particular can be a breeding ground for bacteria, and certain worktop materials are also unsuitable as they are not damp-resistant.

A simple improvement is to replace the worktop in the galley with a modern, brighter, easy to clean material. There are many new solutions to choose from, although some are rather expensive.

Desirable qualities in a worktop:

- Heat-resistant
- Easy to keep clean
- Surface should have raised edges to keep bowls etc. in place
- Comfortable working height (preferably 90–100 cm/36–40 in)

Something to consider when you fit a new worktop is to install an undermount sink, so any water that splashes when you are washing up will run back into the sink. With a top-mounted sink, the water is stopped by the sink's flange and has a tendency to run down into the cool box instead, if one is fitted into the unit. Edge mouldings can be fitted round the lid to the cool box, which will prevent water from trickling into it to a certain degree.

Similarly, you should keep an eye on where the water (or sharp cutting knife, etc.) ends up when the boat is leaning on different tacks. It is unusual for the boat designer to pay any real attention to this. A good and adequately raised edging trim round the work surfaces should stop things from flying around, even when you encounter turbulence while cooking.

Most of us with a boat big enough for a galley probably have a worktop made of laminated plywood board, such as Perstorp. Materials such as these work very well, and they are cheap and easy to work with.

The alternative is stainless plate or one of the new composites, which are becoming increasingly popular on board new boats and are suitable for use in renovation projects. Read more about materials in the facts box.

Left: A typical galley layout in a reasonably modern boat.

Right: In the small sailing boat Cornish Crabber 22, where there is no standing height, the galley has been fitted next to the seat and the working height is compromised. A detachable cushion hides a potential space for a cool box.

TIPS FOR PLANNING A CONVENIENT GALLEY

- **Make a wish-list. Think about what you really want in and from the galley.**
- **Set a budget. Decide how much the galley is allowed to cost.**
- **Get inspiration from functional galleys at a boat show or on board friends' boats.**
- **If you have a choice – make sure to have a good working height for the worktop (90–100 cm/36–40 in).**
- **Make sure that water cannot get into the cool box.**
- **Have good working light directly above the worktop.**
- **It pays to buy good quality materials.**

THE COOKER

The installation of a cooker and perhaps an LP-gas unit also needs some planning. The cooker should preferably have two rings, so you can boil potatoes while frying a steak.

With a small boat, there will almost always have to be a compromise in the galley. If you have a cooker with only one ring, you'll need a little bit more planning when cooking.

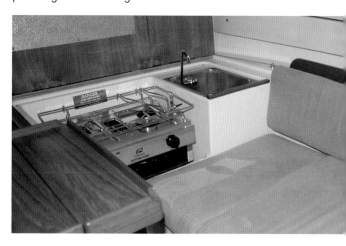

A small portable cooker can also be handy for boiling potatoes on shore, while the steaks and sausages are on the barbecue. This also means you don't have to keep running back to the boat for bits of your supper. A small LP-gas cooker with disposable bottles is also a good emergency standby, if the regular cooker should run out of fuel or break down.

Speaking of fuel, there are cookers for all kinds, but the most common is LP-gas. Then there are spirit stoves, followed by kerosene and diesel stoves. What you choose is merely a matter of preference.

Gimballed suspension can be very useful on a sailing boat, if you anticipate cooking out in the open sea. If you spend most of your time sailing in sheltered areas, it may not be necessary – fiddle rails and pots with high sides may be enough.

STORAGE

Storage is normally the biggest problem for small boats. Usually there are a few drawers for items such as cutlery and a cupboard under the worktop for pots and pans. The pots and pans usually have to share their space with the sink outlet, etc., which makes it a tight fit.

The cabinets above the galley are perhaps the most difficult to design well. Some kind of door to keep things in place is good, and if you can also prevent the crockery and glasses from knocking together, so much the better.

Square, transparent plastic containers, for cereals,

Above, left to right: The continuous edge of the galley worktop in a Luffe 40 creates a guard against falling onto the cooker when the boat lurches.

With a diesel cooker you avoid the need for an open flame. It also works as a heater in this motorboat.

In this system, crockery is kept in place by pegs inserted into a perforated base.

pasta and such, are space-savers. Write the expiry dates on stickers and perhaps cut out the cooking instructions from the packaging and leave in the containers with the contents.

You can also save space by storing in heavy-duty plastic bags (like Ziplock freezer bags), because they never take up more space than their contents and can therefore be stacked easily. Take all unused food items home with you for dry storage during the winter to avoid dampness.

A net attached to the cabin ceiling is ideal for airy storage of fruit and vegetables, so they keep longer. Even better, wrap them in paper and store them in a cool place under the floorboards.

A chopping board that fits onto the sink is simple to make. Sometimes there is space for a folding worktop at the end of the unit, which can be raised and used for someone to help out with chopping vegetables.

Top left: In a 20-ft (6-m) motorboat – in this case a small 21-foot Fjord 21 Weekender motorboat – you really have to use all the tricks in the book to fit a functional galley. This is a renovated area.

Top right: In a bigger boat – this one is a Nauticat 385 with a doghouse – there is plenty of space a half-flight down. Everything is on the same side of the boat.

Below: In this weekend sailboat, a Bénéteau First 25.7, it has been possible to squeeze in a mini-galley with the essential features.

Bottom and centre left: The super compact kitchen in a 7.5 metre long Dutch Sunhorse 25 – all features have two or even three functions. The diesel stove has a lid with a fan and also serves as a heater. The unit to the front of the galley also has two functions and can be used as a table to sit around, or pulled out to sit on while cooking.

Left, top to bottom: The clever U-shaped galley design in a Hallberg-Rassy 31 provides support from behind you when you are cooking in choppy seas. There are two taps, one for pressurised water from the fresh-water tank and one that lets in sea water via a foot pump. The sinks are positioned close to the centre line of the boat, an advantage when the boat is leaning.

The galley in this medium-sized modern racing boat, the Bénéteau First 27.7, occupies very little space. The sink is close to the centre line and drains even when the boat is heeling.

A modern galley on board a Hanse boat, but it is virtually impossible to cook in rough seas.

Below: A folding or swivelling tap can be pushed down so you can place a lid over the galley or open a cupboard door more easily.

In many motorboats, a super-compact galley module fitted beneath the passenger seat saves space. A metal sheet under the seat protects against the heat after use.

On this Corsair 28, the whole galley is located in the afterdeck. Perfect when the weather is good, and when the weather changes for the worse you just pull the cover over.

SINKS

A sink has either one or two bowls. If you only have one, you can rinse in a plastic bowl or wash up first, then rinse. Washing up is simpler with two bowls, but they take up a lot more space. If you have a sailing boat, a good location for the sink is near the boat's centre line – you can wash up when the boat is leaning and the water still runs out. The sink bowls should also be deep enough for the water to stay in place – about 20 cm (8 in) is ideal, but may be hard to find.

Sinks are normally made of stainless steel, but composite sinks are now available to fit invisibly into a worktop of the same material.

WATER

Pressurised water is common on modern boats and just as convenient as at home – you just turn on the tap and there is water. If you also have a water heater, life is even easier. The disadvantage with pressurised water is that it uses a lot of fresh water, since you tend to run the water a little longer than needed; and the pump is often noisy enough to wake everyone on the boat (and sometimes the neighbouring boats) if someone wants to wash their hands after a late loo visit. Pressurised water is easy to install as an afterthought, if you want that kind of 'luxury' on board.

A foot or hand pump is more economical with the fresh water and makes a tank of drinking water last longer. A foot pump for sea water is a good complement.

WASTE

In many boats, finding a suitable place for the waste bin is not a simple task if you want something more permanent than a plastic bag hanging on a hook somewhere. Most boats have a steel wire basket fixed to the inside of a cabinet door, although there are designs where you lift a lid in the worktop and scrape food waste and other rubbish into a bin below.

If you have space, you can fit a pull-out holder with three plastic containers for sorting waste on board. That way you do your bit for the environment and you can throw the bags with organic waste into a waste container before they get smelly. Glass and cans you can take back home with you.

THE FRIDGE

Should you have a fridge or cool box? A fridge cabinet with a door is suitable for motorboats, as there is plenty of space. It is more convenient as you have easy access to the contents.

However, a cool box retains the cold more efficiently and the food stays in place better, even during a choppy crossing. A fridge is normally supplied as a 'package' ready to install and connect the power, whereas a box often needs to be custom-built to fit the particular shape of the boat in an optimal way.

VENTILATION

Medium-sized boats often have their galley by the entrance, which makes for good air circulation and the possibility of talking to people in the cockpit or on the bridge. Opening vents above the galley are the most effective way to get rid of cooking smells. It is not very nice when the whole interior smells of cooking all evening.

Top: The inside of the fridge is made of plastic-coated stainless steel, which makes cleaning easy. A useful basket can easily be lifted out, allowing quicker access and a shorter time for the lid to be open.

A sunken lid in the galley countertop makes it easy for water and dirt to gather in the corners. It provides a sleek surface, but is not very practical.

PRACTICAL TIPS FOR THE BLUE WATER CRUISER'S GALLEY

■ Put silicon cord around the bottom of plates and cups. Press lightly against a base covered in clingfilm/wax paper. It is a good way to stop things slipping.

■ Make a holder for a non-corrosive thermos flask, which is filled with hot water in the morning. It can then be used to make tea, instant coffee or hot chocolate during the day.

■ Eat food out of bowls (the type with a suction base, designed for dogs or toddlers) – it is easier when the waves are rolling.

■ If you are on a long sea crossing, you can eat out of a plastic food flask with a large opening, which you hang round your neck on a strap. That way you can eat with

one hand and hold on with the other. Should you suddenly have to do something, the food will still be there, under your chin.

■ Make a full-length apron out of waxed cloth. Stitch on a pocket at the bottom for good (although not complete) protection against boiling water when cooking in rough seas. Boots and wet weather gear offer better protection, but can get intolerably hot.

■ On a smaller boat, you can warm water for washing up (and for showering) in a purpose-bought black shower bag, hanging in the sun and catching the rays during the day.

■ You can wash up in sea water, but cutlery and Teflon-coated pans should be rinsed in fresh water to avoid staining.

FOCUS FUNCTIONALITY ABOVE ALL

Between 1992 and 2005, four 10-month-long Global Challenge round-the-world charity races took place in a fleet of identical boats, each sailed by a paying crew of 18 under very tough conditions. On board the 22-m (72-ft) steel cruisers used for the 2000/2001 and 2004/2005 races, the shared living space was minimal (albeit not as spartan as the Volvo Ocean Race boats – the crew on the Global Challenge did after all pay to sail!), with nothing but the absolute essentials on board.

However, everything underwent thorough testing over the decade or so when these boats were used for the race, and it was the galley in a Global Challenge boat that provided the inspiration for *Roobarb*'s new galley. It is good that it is bright and easy to care for with durable surfaces, and that function comes before appearance.

Above: The galley is a U-shape, so you have support when the boat lurches heavily. The stainless steel surfaces are practical, as are the raised edges that stop the food ending up on the floor when the sea is choppy.

The stainless steel sink has very deep sides and is almost central in the boat, so that the water will drain even when the boat heels.

Right: The galley has plenty of cabinets and raised-edge worktops where things can be safely placed for storage even when the waves are high.

A BRAND NEW GALLEY

If the galley in your boat is old and tatty, or perhaps just not functional, you can adapt, change or renovate it. On board *Roobarb* we built a brand new galley from scratch, after planning and research.

Roobarb's galley had definitely seen better days. Although some parts were made of solid mahogany, the chipboard worktop had been exposed to splashes from washing-up water and was far from clean. You could easily insert a screwdriver deep into the board, so a project priority was to replace it with something more hygienic.

The worktop was also of a dark brown laminate, which made the whole galley feel more dreary and cramped than it actually was.

*The galley on **Roobarb** before (above) and after (below) the renovation.*

MORE THAN INTENDED

The original idea was to limit the project to replacing the worktop and installing a new stainless sink with two bowls. A couple of years earlier I had painted some surfaces in the galley a pale colour, but had not done anything to the decayed worktop.

As soon as I embarked on dismantling the galley, I realised it would be hard to salvage since parts were glued together, and I had to use the saw.

The main pine carcass was in quite good condition, but the water pumps had been screwed into the hull stringers (reinforcements along the hull with balsa wood in the centre), which had resulted in some damp damage.

Since *Roobarb* is built for two people, with only two berths in its 8-m (27-ft) space, there is room for a huge galley in relation to the size of the boat.

I thought the layout of the old galley worked well, with the cooker (an old English kerosene Taylor 030 with two rings, grill, and an oven) at the very back of the stern and a cabinet about 110 cm (43 in) wide, with plenty of space for food and cooking equipment.

After a few weeks of pondering and lots of research for the right things, the practical work could commence one grey and cold October day.

WORK ROUTINE

Unscrewing, sawing and prising off the old galley took only about an hour. The mouldings glued to the hull were removed with the help of the Multimaster saw's finest and most flexible blade. Then, using a wire-brush attached to the angle grinder, I made an attempt to remove decades of old embedded dirt (or at least old, soft paint).

I used the dimensions from the previous galley solely so that I could hang on to the old kerosene stove for the new galley. I didn't want to replace it with an LP-gas cooker at the moment.

I designed the new galley based on inspiration from a Global Challenge boat, with easy-to-clean surfaces and fairly clean lines, which I think look best and are very practical.

The end result gave the impression of an almost entirely plastic galley, with a prominent rounded corner, a tough, painted surface in two-component paint, and a practical composite worktop.

REFERENCE POINT

Because it is hard to locate an even, horizontal line on a boat in storage in a marina with a sloping harbour ground, you have to find a compromise as close to what you think (or, at best, can estimate) the horizontal lines to be – both longitudinal and transverse.

On *Roobarb* I chose to use the doorpost of the main bulkhead (installed at the boatyard) as a reference point. It turned out to be a few degrees out from the original galley, but that did not really matter. If a worktop is not horizontal, the water cannot run off and could collect in a corner. But a boat at sea is never still, so it is not that important.

A small boat is always impacted by waves and how it is loaded.

A CLEVERLY ROUNDED CORNER

It occurred to me that a sharp edge just below the ladder could be the cause of many bruises, so I decided to make the corner of the galley rounded. It proved a bit tricky, but the end result was excellent, despite the dead space created by the rounded corner.

Eventually, I will make some specially adapted mini-shelves, with sturdy wire guards to hold small bottles and jars.

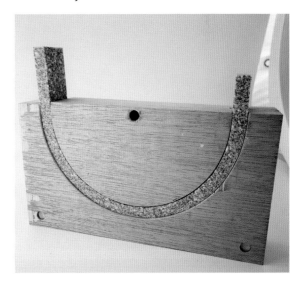

One challenge of the project was to bend an edge trim for the worktop, which is almost as hard as stone.

DOUBLE BOWL SINK

In the old galley I had a double-bowl sink, which is very convenient, if you have the space. I also wanted extra deep stainless bowls, preferably 20 cm (8 in) deep, and I eventually tracked these down at an Italian manufacturer. Extra deep bowls are good when the boat is leaning when you are sailing and you still want to be able to wash up. If you sail across open seas, deep sink bowls are an absolute must, in my opinion.

COOL BOX

On the opposite side of the galley, under the new bench, I fitted the cool box. There is a step-by-step guide to fitting this on pages 103–5.

The sink outlet was replaced with a combined outlet and heat exchanger, to cool the compressor. The new sink meant I also had to move the outlet 30 cm (12 in) so it would be positioned centrally underneath the drain hole.

I filed the old hole down to about 10 cm (4 in) all round (chamfering of about 1:10 is just right; a 5 mm/0.2 in thick hull gives a finished surface with a radius of just under 50 mm/2 in). Then I used 7–8 coats of epoxy glue and woven glass cloth, cut into circles of increasing diameter, to cover the hole.

I plastered, sanded and painted the repair work when I painted the rest of the hull side with two-component paint.

WORKTOP

I like to experiment with different materials that are not so common in boats. Therefore the new dinette is made out of Forex, which is foam PVC but equivalent to plywood when it comes to working with and using it.

I chose a composite worktop, and looked at the materials increasingly used by the boatyards in order to get a predictable and perfect finish to the bathroom and the galley.

THE DINETTE

I rebuilt the dinette a few years ago. I will not go into the detail of this in this book, but essentially I replaced a bench along one side where you either had to sit next to each other to eat or use an extra folding chair.

Now you sit opposite each other and, if necessary, you can seat three or four people at the table. What is lacking is good lighting for the table, and I am still searching for a good solution.

LOOKING AHEAD

I think the galley on board a boat is something many people want to replace, just like the kitchen and toilet in a new flat or house when you move in, to get a fresh start and put your own mark on these rooms.

I have deliberately made quite simple changes and it takes no time, with paint and new cushion covers, to get a completely new feel to the interior. At present I am really happy with the result, although there are still a few minor details to take care of.

PROJECT LOG

TIME: approx. 80 hours.

SKILL LEVEL: medium (the worktop made it harder).

COST: approx. £600.

1

▲ The old galley was partly repainted a few years ago, but still worn. It was time to do something about it before undertaking long-distance sailing.

2

▲ You can see the 30-year-old double sink was rusty and had been repaired in a few places.

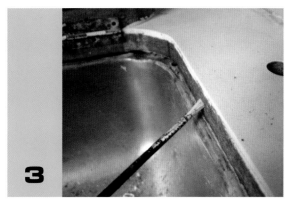

3

▲ The old worktop, made of laminate on fibreboard, had absorbed washing-up water over the years and gone quite soft.

4

▲ What started out as a worktop replacement ended up with the whole galley being replaced.

5

▲ The old material had been thoroughly secured with screws and glue, and I had to use a saw to remove various parts.

6

▲ Using the special blade on the Fein Multimaster, I simply sawed off the mouldings that were glued to the hull.

▲ Most of the old galley has gone. It is time to start rebuilding it.

▲ Using a water-jet cutter, I cut out the worktop and the galley front and doors according to my computer drawings. See the separate box on page 87 for more details.

▲ I had to determine a reference point around which to build the rest of the galley. I finally opted for the doorpost of the main bulkhead.

▲ The front is in place and adjusted with a grinder to fit the curved hull. There were many adjustments before I was happy with it.

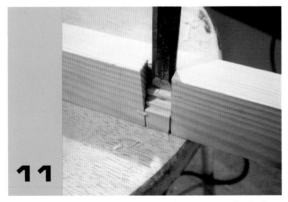

▲ New mouldings for the top edge against the hull were cut to follow the hull side. Indentations were made to accommodate the sides of the galley.

▲ The indentations in the back moulding held the side pieces in place while they were tested and adjusted to fit the curved hull.

13

▲ The sides were shaped roughly using the side panels of the old galley as a guide. A more precise shape was made using a pencil and compass.

14

▲ An abrasive belt grinder with 40-grade sandpaper was used to rough-finish the shape of the side panels over and over again, until I was happy with the fit against the hull and front.

15

▲ I put the pieces together a few times to check the fit. Here they are with the water-jet cut worktop in Corian.

16

▲ A carpenter helped me make the galley corner out of beech. First, two pieces were glued together to make a corner.

17

▲ Then the rounded shape was finished with a planing machine.

18

▲ Finally, the carpenter did the fine planing by hand.

19

▲ I tried the corner piece in place and measured the adjustment needed at the bottom to fit against the curved hull.

20

▲ A template of the hull was made out of cardboard and transferred to the corner piece.

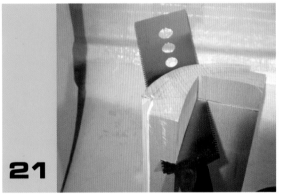

21

▲ The piece was cut to fit the rounded hull with a Japanese saw – it wasn't right the first time, and I had to cut off a little bit more.

22

▲ I primed the corner piece to distinguish more easily where it needed to be sanded. The result had to be completely round.

23

▲ The galley sides were filleted against the hull with epoxy and then reinforced with woven glass tape.

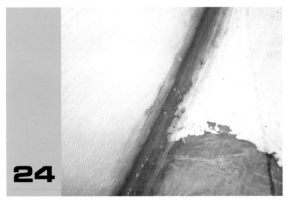

24

▲ The epoxy glue was mixed with brown thickener (silica), which gives it the reddish brown colour in the picture.

25

▲ First, I used a few coats of primer (two-component) to get a smooth paint surface.

26

▲ I wanted the galley's exterior surface to be smooth, and that required several coats of primer, since the plywood did not have a very good surface to start with.

27

▲ The surface was sanded with 120-grade sandpaper between each coat – there were four coats of paint in the end. A heater helped against the cold (below zero) outside the shed.

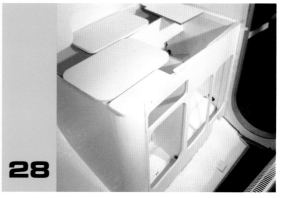

28

▲ The doors also needed to be primed on both sides – with the sanding between each coat, it took about a week before the priming was complete.

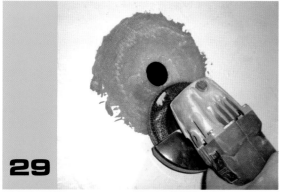

29

▲ Because of the new sink bowls, the outlet and hull piping had to be moved. The edges of the old outlet hole were chamfered 1:10 with a grinder.

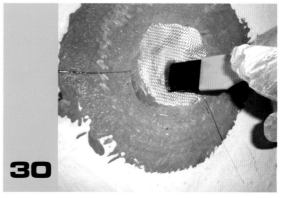

30

▲ Circles of woven glass cloth of increasing diameter were saturated with epoxy to form a new laminate of the same thickness as the old one.

▲ Board templates of all the shelves were made and rough-sawn.

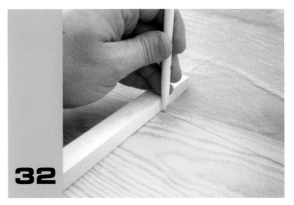

▲ The rounded shape of the hull was transferred to the back edges of the shelves (easiest to do with a compass, but this method works) and then sawn.

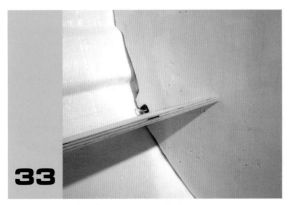

▲ Most of the shelves are angled to keep the pots and pans in place when the boat lurches. A trim on the outer edge is the final touch.

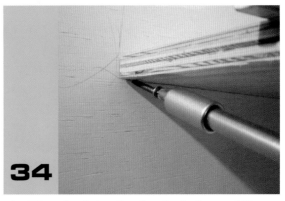

▲ When the shelves fitted perfectly they would be fixed with epoxy glue. First, I made temporary supports of thin screws, to keep them in place when gluing.

▲ All edges to be glued were first saturated with unthickened epoxy and then epoxy filleted.

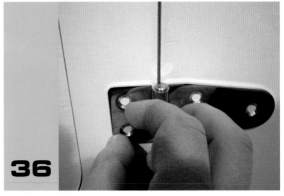

▲ Stainless hinges are fitted onto all three doors. It was not very easy to get them to open perfectly, and I tried it out on scrap pieces of plywood first.

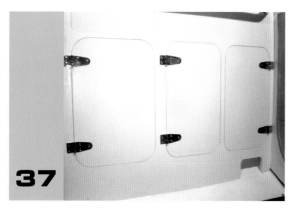

37

▲ Water-jet cutting means the doors can be cut from the same piece of plywood as the front piece, and therefore fit perfectly, with a 2-mm (0.08-in) gap.

38

▲ At the top edge I drilled holes for a stainless steel handhold, which will prove to be very useful in choppy seas.

39

▲ The handhold is secured from the inside with 8-mm (0.3-in) bolts and large washers, which cannot be seen from the outside.

40

▲ Finally, Jenni the stylist could put all her things in place and make it look attractive for the photos.

The renovation was a real success!

FOCUS DIFFERENT WORKTOP MATERIALS

COMPOSITE

Corian is a well-known example of composite material made up of mineral bound together by acrylic plastic, which together with colouring agents can resemble stone or just be plain. The composite boards come in hundreds of colour combinations.

Composite materials can resist most things, except ballpoint pens and certain solvents. Most stains can be removed simply by polishing, but tougher stains can be rubbed off materials with an abrasive scourer.

The DIY disadvantage with these boards is that they require special glue, which you can only get hold of through the trade. It is possible to use ordinary woodworking tools, but the margins are smaller and in retrospect I can only say that it was not particularly easy – I had to throw away the first board, for instance, because it was damaged during the water-jet cutting. Of course, damages can be fixed, but it was easier to buy a new board since, as always, I was also short of time.

Composite only needs quite a simple frame underneath to give enough support. It does not need to be glued to a board. Corian is not cheap, about £100–190 per metre (39 in) board, (70 cm/28 in wide). Then there is the added labour cost, roughly £40–60 per hour, so the price per board can easily rocket if you want rounded mouldings or glued sink bowls.

There are alternatives of the same type: HI-MACS, Lyrec and Evante are other worktop materials.

Corian and similar products come in more than a hundred colour combinations, from plain to imitation stone and fantasy patterns. This is the galley in a Nauticat 385.

LAMINATE

Of the laminates, Perstorp is probably the best known. In ordinary kitchens the laminate is glued onto fibreboard, but on board it is better glued onto waterproof plywood.

If the worktop is thin, it is best to glue laminate onto the bottom as well, so the plywood does not warp.

STAINLESS STEEL

Stainless steel is very tough, but it may become expensive if you need to weld and bend the sheet. The easiest way is to glue it onto water- and boil-proof (WBP) plywood. Bending it, for example to get an angled back edge, costs about £20 from a workshop. If you want to cut it yourself, you can use an angle grinder.

Laminate comes in many colours and can look like solid wood, if that is the style you want. This galley is in a Degerö 27.

Stainless steel is tough. Bend the edges to prevent water from getting under the mouldings. This galley is in a Luffe 40.

FOCUS   WATER-JET CUTTING

WATER-JET CUTTING

When you do your own design, you can come up with some sophisticated solutions with the help of water-jet or laser cutting.

What you need is a computer-generated cutting template in a vector format (you can do this in a CAD programme or a drawing programme, such as Adobe Illustrator or CorelDRAW). If you cannot do it yourself, there are companies that can help.

In my case, I wanted to cut rather than mill, because the thin cuts make it possible to use the cut-out windows as well. For composite, the next best thing to use is a hand-held milling machine, whereas a keyhole saw can cause tension in the board and cause it to crack, according to the professionals.

The water-jet cuts as if through butter with 4000 bar pressure in the jet and blasting sand. In less than ten minutes the boards were ready, both the composite and the plywood. I also had a few pieces of 5-mm (0.2-in) stainless steel cut (for a new rudder design) and that was also done really quickly and easily.

Water-jet cutting can be used for a lot of things, especially for complex shapes like my rounded doors. The best thing about it is that it is fairly easy to get a good result.

Right: I made my own full-scale cutting drawing in a computer program (for vector graphics). I had measured the rounded shape of the hull (and I consequently had to sand down some of the board in situ).

The professional configuring the cutting machine, having converted my vector image to CAD format on his own computer.

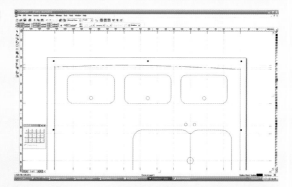

The first composite board had craters where the jet went through. You resolve that by starting outside the line. That is what we did on the second board...

The front of the galley, in 12 mm (0.5 in) lauan plywood, was quick to cut. If it is not going to be painted, be sure to rinse the board carefully immediately after cutting it.

Even the hard composite was easy to cut, once we knew to start outside the cutting line.

FOCUS | MAKING A ROUND CORNER

A prerequisite for the fairly generous curve of one of the worktop corners is the capability to mould the material for the edging. It proved easier than I expected. Corian (and probably the other similar materials from competitors), when heated to 175°C (350°F) for 10 minutes, becomes flexible and easy to mould.

The jig was built using several layers of plywood and a tabletop milling machine. The groove was cut using a cutting blade that matched the thickness of the Corian (12 mm/0.5 in).

The most important thing I learned from this part of the project was to use edge moulding that was longer and deeper than required, then grind it to the right shape once it had been moulded to the right radius. It was hard to avoid it distorting a little, and the result was the same for all the test pieces.

I ran several tests on bending the composite in the oven in my flat, to find the best way to do it. The third moulded piece came out almost perfect after 10 minutes, but I did a couple more, just to test the method.

These pieces of Corian were fixed with hot-melt adhesive to act as support to the edge piece, primarily to stop the edge piece sliding on the base and leaving glue stains on the surface. When they have hardened they are almost impossible to get off, except with a mortise chisel.

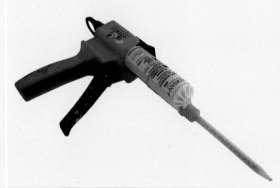

This glue, which is a two-component type, is strong and requires a little practice before using. The mixer gun needs to be changed between each gluing session, as the glue hardens inside within a few minutes.

Use plenty of clamps when gluing composite material.

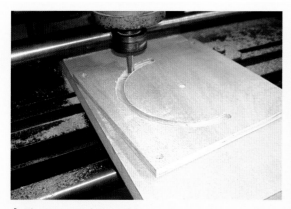

1 The jig is made out of several layers of plywood, milled to the correct radius.

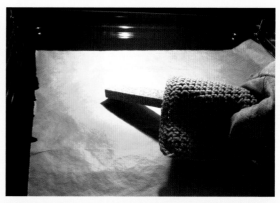

2 Preheat the oven to 175°C (375°F), then put the piece in the oven on a tray for 10 minutes. Use oven gloves and a pot-holder when you take it out of the oven.

3 The piece is quite soft after baking in the oven and can easily be moulded into shape on the jig and held in place with clamps for 15 minutes while cooling.

4 The piece is cut to the right length and the edges sanded until completely flat, using a long piece of sandpaper glued onto a piece of plywood.

5 Before the glue has hardened completely, it must be carefully removed with a very sharp mortise chisel.

6 The new corner moulding is glued on last, using lots of clamps, and is then carefully sanded down to match the height of the straight edge mouldings. Done!

FOCUS PROFESSIONALS WORKING

PROFESSIONALS WORKING WITH CORIAN

Calle Garderyd works with Corian every day and he advised me how to do this project. Calle's company mostly makes interiors for kitchens, but occasionally he gets requests from boat owners for worktops.

1 Calle uses the same tools as for wood. The boards are cut to shape using a blade with a very specific denticulation.

2 The pre-cut pieces of Corian, with cut-off corners, are glued to the board with hot-melt glue as support for the moulding during the gluing process.

3 A special two-component glue is used once the surfaces have been sanded a little and thoroughly de-greased.

4 The glue should be smoothed evenly outwards from the joint. Excess glue is removed with a sharp chisel before it hardens completely (approx. 10–15 minutes).

5 The sink is glued on underneath using mouldings of Corian with a milled corner the same thickness as the stainless steel sheet of the sink.

>> TRIPLED STORAGE

In a motorboat with an interior that was basically good, but with a galley that did not work for the family's boating holidays, Jakob Magnusson created a brand-new design.

Jakob's motorboat, a Norwegian Comet 31 Commander, built from a kit in 1982, had an interior that was adequate as far as the cabins went, as they seemed to have been installed by a professional boat carpenter. The existing galley, however, was not as well designed. There were insufficient work surfaces, the working height was low and storage was lacking, which meant the family had to keep food in baskets on the deck when they spent time on the boat.

Jakob spent a few summers pondering how he wanted things and sought inspiration from boat shows, taking photographs with a digital camera and studying brochures.

He started by thinking about how he used the galley in the boat, comparing it to the kitchen at home. At home, he had plenty of handy surfaces and they were a good working height for the back, at 90 cm (35 in).

He also considered whether moving the driving seat, the bulkheads or anything else on board would offer a better way of optimising the existing space.

The galley before the renovation (above), and the end result (below).

Using a CAD program, Jakob made a drawing that included all the ideas and functions he wanted. 'But remember, if you are going to make any changes it is important to consider the boat's stability,' says Jakob.

DRAWING AND CALCULATING

Once Jakob had looked at how he wanted the galley from all possible angles, and even taken into account how big the cooker and fridge would be, his plan was ready. The equipment he chose was a single round sink, rather than a double, as it would leave more workspace. He usually used a separate bowl for rinsing anyway. The cooker he opted for was a two-ring top-mounted gas stove, with space for large frying pans. Jakob found that many stoves with lids had limited cooking space. He decided to do without an oven, since the cookers with a built-in oven available on the market didn't appeal to him.

THE JOB

Jakob started by cutting out the drawer fronts at home in the garage. His advice is to make sure you have absolutely straight and linear cutting lines, and warns that the existing edges on plywood boards may not be straight enough to be used as they are.

A large-scale carpenter's square was a good help. The fronts and visible areas of the casing were made of teak-veneered boil-proof plywood, while the hidden surfaces were made of cheaper lauan plywood, also boil-proof.

All visible edges were covered in veneer mouldings, attached with hot-melt glue, to hide the plywood

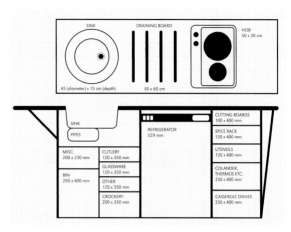

It helps to do a good drawing, to be sure that everything fits, before you start cutting into the boat.

edges. All the drawers had special runners, which were supplied with clear instructions and were not particularly hard to assemble. A special aluminium trim was tailor-made for the drawer locks to have something to lock against.

The worktops and the hull behind the galley were veneered with laminate and holes were cut out for the cooker and sink.

THE END RESULT

Jakob is very happy with the end result: 'Our available storage in the galley has tripled and we now have functional surfaces for working and putting things on,' he says, and adds that it took about 200 hours of labour, which includes making the drawers in the garage at home.

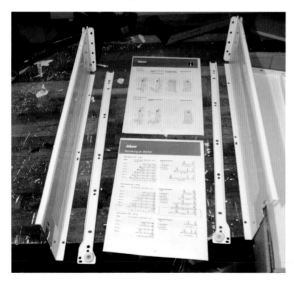

The drawers roll easily on runners and are the same type as used by some boatbuilders in their galley interiors.

PROJECT LOG

SKILL LEVEL: medium.

COST: estimated cost for everything, including fridge, cooker, etc., approx. £2400. This is a fairly extensive project (three units with 14 drawers); a smaller galley may be considerably cheaper and faster to build.

TIME: estimated 150–200 hours.

▲ Jakob used a 12-mm (0.5-in) thick double-sided teak plywood for the drawer fronts. The grains are matched so they are in the 'right position' in the stack of drawers.

▲ The drawer fronts are edged with teak moulding, which is attached by heating it with an iron and pressing on it with a wood block. It is particularly important to make sure the ends stick properly.

▲ Most of the excess moulding was removed with a DIY-planer. The rest was sanded down with 80-grade and 150-grade sandpaper along the veins of the veneer.

▲ The casing of the unit is made of 12-mm (0.5-in) plywood. The corners were reinforced with pine trim fixed with screws every 10 cm (4 in).

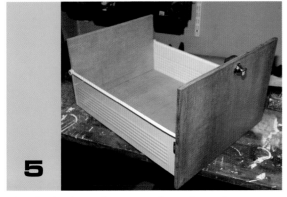

▲ The back panels were made to almost the same height as the front panels, to avoid the problem of things slipping down behind the drawers. 9-mm (0.35-in) lauan is suitable for this purpose.

▲ For the lock, a hole of 27 mm (1.06 in) was drilled, so that the top of the locking cylinder is in line with the top of the drawer front. Then the locking cylinder was centred, with the knob and backplate in place.

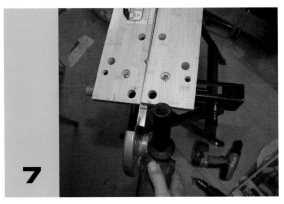

7 ▲ An L-shaped 15-mm (0.6-in) aluminium trim 2-mm (0.08-in) thick was cut to make a tongue, into which two screw holes were drilled.

8 ▲ The tongue was bent to a 90° angle (don't bend too hard!) and fixed with screws in the outer shell, using the drawer as a template.

9 ▲ When measuring where to fit the runners, it is important to leave a little bit of space for the aluminium trim for the drawer above.

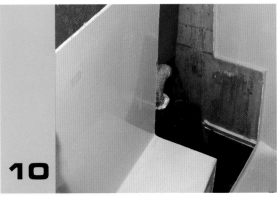

10 ▲ Some of the inner lining is cut away to make more space for the new galley layout, and then a piece of plywood is glued onto it as a base for the new galley.

11 ▲ A heat gun, held at the appropriate distance, helps the glue to harden in cold weather.

12 ▲ The raw glass-fibre surface of the inside of the hull is smoothed down with a glass-fibre spatula, using a Plastic Padding glass-fibre filler.

13

▲ A laminate panel was glued on with Ceresit PL600 adhesive applied with a tooth spatula, to act as a splash guard. The new pipes for the inlet and exhaust for the heater can be seen at the bottom.

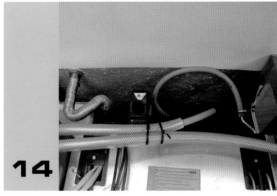

14

▲ The liquid gas was supplied with a shut-off tap adjacent to the galley. The supply hoses are placed inside thicker hoses to protect them from wear and tear.

15

▲ The worktop was made out of 15-mm (0.6-in) birch plywood with white laminate glued to it. The teak moulding strips (available from most chandleries) were glued with PL600.

16

▲ A store cupboard or food store with pull-out drawers was fitted under the driver's seat. White laminate was glued onto the carcass with PL600.

17

▲ A battery provided the required pressure during the drying process.

18

▲ To create an attractive frame for the top surface of the store cupboard, a teak edge trim was specially milled and then glued with PL600.

19

▲ The store cupboard is also the driver's seat – the bench was mounted onto a separate plywood board with runners, so the driving position can be adjusted.

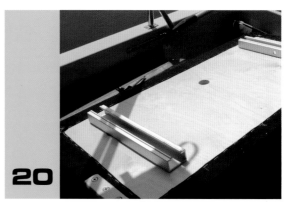

20

▲ Corresponding runners are fitted to the base of the double seat.

21

▲ The store cupboard is secured with screws to a joining surface against the inner lining. Later on, this area will also house fuses and switches for the electrical system.

22

▲ The new 85-cm (33-in) wide double seat, clad in Sunbrella cushion fabric, in place on top of the store cupboard. The seat is mounted on hinges and can be tipped forwards.

23

▲ A new unit for the dinette was also made out of 12-mm (0.5-in) teak plywood, framed by a teak edge trim with a milled groove. The legs were attached with hinges.

24

▲ The solution with runners for the drawers turned out better than expected. One drawer had space for three bins – useful for empties, for example.

▲ The store cupboard under the driver's seat is ready and has a new worktop. A new bench is fitted to the back of the store cupboard unit.

▲ With a 103-litre (22.5-gal) liquid-gas-powered fridge, there is no need for batteries and it gets properly cold. The contents are for celebrating during a trip with the lads!

JAKOB'S BEST TIPS

■ Take a digital camera and visit a boat show. Go through the boats systematically and look for smart solutions, dimensions that seem suitable, etc.

Take lots of pictures, preferably with a tape measure included. That will give you a lot of dimensions automatically! Jakob took hundreds of pictures at the boat show before the renovation.

■ A search for 'galley' on the internet can also bring inspiration. Steal ideas from the luxury yachts!

■ Start by giving the plywood boards one coat of varnish. This will make it easier to remove any glue residue, which can otherwise be hard to get off. Mark all pieces 'in' or 'out' and 'up' or 'down' with masking tape, to save time and avoid wondering how the pieces fit together.

■ When pre-drilling plywood, cut off the drill tip so it will not accidentally go all the way through the board.

■ If you want, you can use clear wood stain on the lauan plywood, just before varnishing, then the tone will be closer to teak. You can, for example, experiment with teak powder base, diluted with slightly more water so you can apply several coats until you are happy with the tone.

■ To achieve straight, neat, linear cuts in the plywood, without a professional band saw, measure the cutting line with a large carpenter's square. Secure a long spirit level with clamps and measure against the cutting line with the keyhole saw you are using.

Use a good-quality keyhole saw, with a fine blade for wood. Use the pendular function on setting 1, and if your keyhole saw has guides, activate them. Let the saw work through by itself, applying very light pressure. Change the blade before it becomes too worn, otherwise it may start to drag. The cutting line you have drawn in advance will help you to monitor that it is really straight. Alternatively, get a professional carpenter to cut the boards perfectly right-angled.

>> BUILD A COOL BOX

Making your own cool box is not that difficult, if you have a little spare space somewhere on board. We make a well-insulated box, to keep the cold in and the heat out even at the height of summer.

Of course, it is a bit of luxury to be able to sip a cold beer on a sunny deck after a day's sailing, or to have fresh cold milk with your morning cereal.

But, unlike 20–30 years ago, it is a luxury that is not impossible these days – and building a box in an old boat is relatively easy. The crux is in planning the best place to put the box and the cooling unit.

Of course, it is much simpler if you can just install a ready-made fridge in the boat, and for many owners of large sailing boats and motorboats this works fine. But the rest of us with smaller boats really want to maximise every inch of unshapely space, and a homemade cool box is the answer.

INSULATION

The most common problem with cool boxes on board is poor insulation. Anders often comes across badly attached frigolite board on boxes, and heavy power consumption as a result of the poor insulation.

It cannot be pointed out clearly enough that the basic requirement for a cool box to function well is plenty of good insulation! I researched a few possible insulation materials before embarking on building a cool box for *Roobarb*. My first thought was to build a plastic box and fill the surrounding space with polyurethane foam, which is a fairly simple method as the foam fills the available space.

A small cool box of approximately 55 litres (12 gal) will make life more comfortable on board the project boat **Roobarb.**

PROJECT LOG

SKILL LEVEL: medium.

TIME: 8–12 hours.

COST: cooling unit Isotherm 2051SP, £800–900 (often special offers). Insulation approx. £10–20 per board (a total of £100 for *Roobarb*). Then add glue (without solvents), brace for the copper pipes, fittings in brass/bronze and some sealant. In total about £1100.

TOOLS: hole saw for hulls 60 mm (2.4 in), plus 40 mm (1.6 in) for the quick couplings. Japanese saw for the boards.

It is easier to vary the menu if you have a good cooling facility on board.

Unfortunately, I discovered that one-component foam, which is relatively damp sensitive, can absorb moisture over the years, resulting in a reduced insulation capacity.

In the US you can buy specially-made board with vacuum, and thus a good insulation capacity (ten times better than polyurethane), but these are unfortunately very expensive. Otherwise, vacuum panels would have been an exciting material that I would have liked to use for the new box.

Other types of cellular plastic – like EPS (see page 120) or PVC polymer foam – are used in boatbuilding as spacing material for sandwich laminate, and can be found in some chandleries and used as insulation.

But the most common material is what the building trade calls 'ground insulation board', which is easy to cut, comes in various thicknesses and is cheap. This has better insulation properties for the thickness compared to most other common materials. Read more about insulation materials in Chapter 7.

RETAINING THE COLD

A cool box should not be too big and should also be well stocked. It is best to fill it with items that are already cold – bring food from the fridge at home, packed straight into a cool bag. Some items, such as milk, can be frozen and act as an ice block. The taste is affected slightly, but is still better than powdered or long-life milk.

Other products, e.g. frozen chicken, defrost in 24 hours or so, and if you plan your menus these chilled and frozen foods can be a good support to retain the cold in the cool box for the first few days of the holiday.

THE RENOVATION

Roobarb happened to have a convenient space underneath one bench in the dinette, as a result of the renovation of the interior.

The space is easily accessible from the galley, although you have to lift a seat pad to get to the lid. I chose not to install the box in the galley itself, since boxes placed there are often difficult to get to and washing-up water can trickle into the gap by the lid to the box.

The challenge when building the box was to get it to follow the hull shape for maximum capacity. It is important that the box is the correct size. If it is too big, it uses up too much power from the batteries to cool empty space. If it is too small, there is no room for what you want chilled.

The requirements for making short passages at weekends are obviously very different from those for long-distance voyages at sea for several weeks with no possibility of replenishing the food store.

With regard to *Roobarb*, the idea is to be able to sail across the oceans, so I wanted a box of around 50–60 litres (11–13 gal) capacity to keep fresh

All the parts for the water-cooled cooling system.

foods cold and perhaps, on occasion, a big, freshly caught fish. The finished box had a 55.3 litre (12 gal) capacity.

FITTING PROBLEMS

I didn't encounter any real difficulties; the biggest problem was that I did not measure carefully enough. I also learned not to press too hard when using the Japanese saw on the thick insulation boards – the thin blade easily twists, and the cut was not straight.

Since the box is placed under a bench, you can expect that some rather heavy person will sit down right on top of the lid at times, so it must be able to withstand that. I solved this problem by cutting the lid at a 45° angle with the keyhole saw. Apart from that, I made hinges at one side and added a mahogany trim all round. Sealing strips in a two-level stepped format prevents cold air from escaping.

The actual compressor and its accessories were not too hard to fit; I had read the instructions carefully. However, two other problems occurred – one was the curvature of the hull, which meant

I had to use an angled pipe sleeve to get the right angle against the outlet from the sink bowls, and the stainless ball valve added too much to the height.

The other problem was that the special fitting in the galley sink drain hose, along with the compressor, were on the opposite side to the cool box. Having spent a lot of time pondering how to fit the copper pipes and their big quick couplings in a safe place, I finally found a solution – but unfortunately I had to cut into my brand-new galley cabinets.

The evaporator in the cool box should be placed as high up as possible, as cold air is heavier than hot air and fills the box from below. That means it is normally colder at the bottom. That is also why the insulation is extra thick – 15 cm (6 in) – at the base of the box.

COOLING UNIT

When you plan to sail in warm waters, compressor cooling – preferably in conjunction with water cooling – is the best option. The system should have fairly low-energy consumption and be able to cool the whole box to freezing, if required.

Thermoelectric cooling units (also with water cooling) normally work well, but use a little more power for the same cooling effect.

Isotherm is a major supplier of compressor units in Europe and has a good reputation among long-distance sailors. That does not mean that their equipment never breaks down or develops problems, rather that the company is well organised and manages to remedy problems by, for example, despatching spare parts quickly.

The system I had been recommended for *Roobarb*'s planned type of sailing has a water-cooled condenser. The difference between an air- or water-cooled system is that one with an air-cooled condenser is a little cheaper than a water-cooled system, but the latter uses considerably less power, which is what I prioritised in my project.

The power consumption depends largely on the difference in temperature between the condenser, located in a special bushing in the hull, and the evaporator, located inside the cool box and absorbing the air from the box (rather than generating cold, as one might think).

If, for example, it is 25°C (77°F) in the water and 8°C (46°F) in the box, the difference in temperature is 17°C (31°F). The greater the difference, the harder the compressor has to work, and thus it uses more power. The system with a water-cooled evaporator that I fitted uses 2.5 ampere (A), but it does not run constantly and I was advised to consider an average consumption of 0.6 A (14.4 ampere hours per 24 hours).

TOP LOADING

If you have good, thick insulation, the only way heat can enter the cool box is through the lid, therefore you should keep the lid off for as short a time as possible. A deep cool box, where you have to take out most of the contents to reach what you want (which inevitably is at the bottom) is obviously not ideal, but hard to avoid unless you store the food in baskets that you can easily pull out.

Lids are better than doors, since cold air is heavy and does not escape if you have a lid at the top. The lid should also have double sealing joints that close really tightly. One tip is to have magnets that keep the lid in place, with no need for a lock device or clasp to hold it in place.

Ready-made lids for a cooling unit can be bought in the US. This framed lid is from Glacier Bay, based in California, and costs start at $540.

Aluminium trim with sealing strip is a good and functional DIY-method. Complement with PU-foam.

INSULATION

It was not that easy to find information about this and there seems to be a lot of confusion with regard to terminology, even among manufacturers.

Thermal conductivity, or R-value, is the term most commonly used to describe the conductive or insulating properties of the material, although there is apparently more than one way of measuring this.

As far as 'R-value' (resistance to heat flow) is concerned, there is complete unit confusion between

European and American calculations. The Americans use the imperial system and degrees in Kelvin (K), whereas Europeans use the metric system and temperatures in Celsius (°C) or K.

This makes it almost impossible to use R-values in practice, since there is no uniform method for how it should be described. But the general principle is: the higher the value, the better.

In Sweden, insulation capacity is normally measured by thermal conductivity (lambda), which is a material's ability to conduct heat. For a cool box, the ability to conduct heat should be poor and have the lowest possible value. For example, the lambda value for thermal conductivity in the extruded polystyrene cellular plastic (such as Ecoprim or Styrofoam) that I used is approximately 0.034 W/m x K.

AND FINALLY

You can get by perfectly well without a fridge, and I have done so with all my boats until now. Tins, cans and a cool compartment fitted into the keelson below, or a box filled with ice, are absolutely fine for shorter or weekend journeys.

The new bench over the cool box has a space that is just right: 55 x 55 x 90 cm (22 x 22 x 35 in) and it follows the curved hull.

Insulated keelson

A cheaper solution than a fridge is to insulate some of the space in the keelson. Under the floorboards is most often the coolest place on board, partly because warm air rises and cold air falls, but primarily because the water surrounding the outside of the hull cools it.

With the help of a few ice-blocks or frozen cartons of milk, you can go for three or four days before having to stop at an island or harbour grocery store.

The same insulation material can be used as for the cool box. The space in the keelson is probably a lot smaller than any other usable place on board, and thinner insulation panels may be needed. In my case, I also wanted the insulation to follow the curved shape of the hull.

One way to retain cold air longer is to make sure that the cold store is always full.

If you are running out of food, use newspaper to fill out the void in the compartment. Opening the lid as little as possible also helps to keep the cold in.

🔺 I bought ground insulation boards of extruded polystyrene, both 100 mm (4 in) and 50 mm (2 in) thick.

🔺 Cutting the pieces took some time. A Japanese saw worked well although there were lots of tiny blue crumbs!

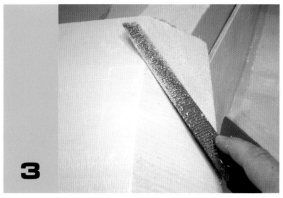

🔺 Using a coarse file, I made some fine adjustments – there were several before the pieces were completely straight.

🔺 As far as possible, I cut or sawed the boards to overlap slightly, to ensure that the insulation covered all gaps.

🔺 The completed box has 50 mm + 100 mm (2 in + 4 in) polystyrene at the bottom, 100 mm (4 in) in the sides and 50 mm (2 in) insulation in the lid.

🔺 All the surfaces were covered with a 3-mm (0.12-in) plastic sheet (Forex), glued in place with plenty of sealant added to the joints.

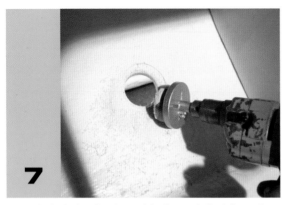

7

▲ The hole for the through-hull was drilled through the hull with a 60-mm (2.4-in) hole drill. I also adjusted its placement by 300 mm (12 in) to fit the new sink.

8

▲ The hole was reinforced with 18-mm (0.7-in) boil-proof, waterproof plywood (WBP), epoxy-glued in place and then painted.

9

▲ The through-hull is fitted from underneath with plenty of sealant and a special zinc anode is added.

10

▲ The evaporator is screwed onto the wall with spacing blocks, placed as high up in the box as possible.

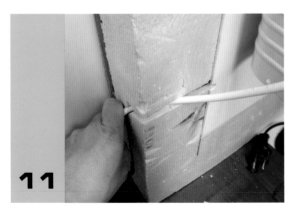

11

▲ The pipe is inserted through the insulation in the groove and over to the other side of the boat.

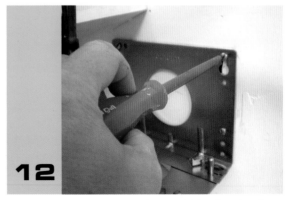

12

▲ The compressor, a Danfoss BD35F, is fitted under the sink, next to the outlet where the airflow is good.

13

▲ The compressor is locked in place with quick-fittings. It has rubber feet to prevent vibrations travelling to the hull and can withstand lurches up to 30°.

14

▲ A power cable 10 mm (4 in) thick is connected to the compressor's junction box straight from the distribution box (the instructions suggested it should be fitted straight from the batteries).

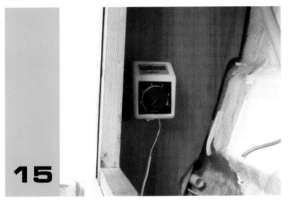

15

▲ I fit the control box in a storage space. I do not anticipate having to change the setting once the cooling unit is set to the correct temperature.

16

▲ The thermostat's sensor for the temperature in the box is fitted to the evaporator.

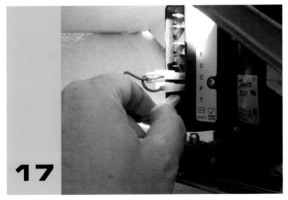

17

▲ The cable from the thermostat is connected to the electronics of the compressor.

18

▲ Done! Now there will be cold, fresh milk for breakfast again!

05
LIGHT AND VENTILATION

>> BRIGHT AND AIRY

Elin Alida is a 46-ft (14-m) steel boat with a bright interior style throughout. It has a white wood trim and details in high-grade wood.

The renowned craftsman Bruce Roberts designed the hull. The first owner, an architect, then designed the deck and interior to his own ideas and needs. Some clever solutions have been tested and in some cases revised – the process has been intense, but now the boat is finally finished. The new owners are going to sail it to the West Indies, and possibly beyond.

The intention with the boat's clean interior style was above all to be able to inspect everything. There are doors and openings for access to all nooks and crannies – especially important on a steel boat.

The interior throughout consists of light surfaces with details in high-grade wood.

Pumps and power cable (almost 3 km/2 miles of cable in total) are also readily accessible. The dining table has a hinged top to make it easy to get to the storage compartments behind without crawling.

FRIDGE IN THE NAVIGATION TABLE

The fridge/freezer is inside the navigation table instead of next to the sink. That way washing-up water cannot trickle into the box and cause bad smells or a frost problem. Even the overflow in the sink has been adjusted to work on all points of sail.

The material for the interior is laminate board in semi-matt white paint. The doorframes are teak, which gives a warmer, cosier feel. This is a style common in American boats.

Anything non-visible in the interior is made out of birch plywood, while the decor in the cabin ceiling and the hull sides is white-painted double-sided tongue and groove pine.

All berth sides are of solid iroko, a high-grade wood that resembles teak.

Opposite: The heads is directly below the window for good lighting and ventilation. Outside the door the diesel heater is just visible.

EASY EVEN WHEN THE SEAS ARE ROLLING

The designer has also taken into account the boat's functionality while sailing. There are handles in all strategic places. Another carefully planned detail is that all lids can be opened with one hand, without the pads getting in the way. This means you can rummage through the berth compartments and hang on at the same time, which may be necessary when the waves are rolling.

Elin Alida

Length: *14 m (46 ft)*
Beam: *4 m (13 ft)*
Draft: *2.4 m (7 ft 10 in)*
Weight: *20 tonnes*
Engine: *75 hp Ford*
Built: *1984–2005*

There are six berths in three cabins. All the berths have good natural light and individual lights above them.

>> BETTER LIGHTING IN THE BOAT

Good lighting is just as important in the boat as at home and at work. Many older boats have a fluorescent tube in the cabin ceiling as the main light source, with perhaps a kerosene lamp for ambiance at dinner. But there are plenty of ways to make the boat both functional and cosy, without using up power unnecessarily. Here are some tips.

Many older boats have too few light sources in the cabin to enable cooking, or reading charts or a good book without risking tired eyes. However, the concept of interiors with a variety of lighting is now common in leisure boats, having been something considered merely for traditional spaces. The focus is mainly on using different types of light sources to make the working environment as efficient as possible, but consideration is also given to enhancing the interior and making it cosier.

The best way of achieving efficient lighting in the boat is to abandon the ordinary ceiling fluorescent tube and divide the light sources into different needs: work light, cooking light, cosy light, etc.

It may seem unnecessary to have several lights that perhaps use more power, but most lights are not on for any length of time during the day, and consumption is kept fairly low by having the right lighting for the purpose. With age, our eyes' ability to adapt to poor light diminishes, so that stronger and

Several small light sources in the cabin make it easier to adapt the light according to need and can be a way of saving energy.

There are many different types of light fittings on the market to meet a variety of needs.

preferably whiter light is needed to read a book or take on any fiddly jobs.

COLOUR TEMPERATURE

Light is normally described in different colour temperatures. Daylight is usually blue (which a fluorescent tube may also be), whereas a light bulb gives off a yellowish-red light. Colour temperature is measured in Kelvin (K).

Daylight has a temperature of 5200 K, whereas a candle has 1900 K and a light bulb has 2800 K. A clear blue sky can have a colour temperature of as much as 11,000 K. Daylight lamps (for example white light-emitting diodes and halogen lights) can be perceived as having a cold blueish light in a cabin.

Our eyes are good at adapting and we normally do not experience this phenomenon clearly. However, in a digital camera you can sometimes see that the image is very discoloured because of light coming from a source that the camera is not focused on. Work light should be as white as possible, which you get from halogen bulbs and light-emitting diodes, whereas a warm light is better for a cosy dinner.

WHAT DOES THE EXPERT SAY?

Boat designer and artist Pelle Lundgren thinks you should investigate new technology to see what benefits that can offer. He mentions light-emitting diodes and fibre optics as possible solutions for onboard interiors: 'The development has progressed very quickly – in just a few years new technology has made it possible to have interesting and practical lighting,' says Pelle.

AMBIENT LIGHTING

Good work light needed for cooking, for example, can be achieved with a halogen bulb to provide a single white light with low energy consumption. Good work light should normally be available at all times, but it is sufficient if it is on when needed. Otherwise, a fluorescent tube provides enough general light.

FOCUS LIGHT

A small spotlight can be used to enhance a decorative object such as a picture hanging on the bulkhead.

READING LIGHT

An adjustable spotlight on the bulkhead is also suitable for reading. The disadvantage is that it gets very hot and therefore must not be fitted close to anything flammable. These days LED lights with very low energy consumption may also be suitable for use on board.

OTHER LIGHT SOURCES

A traditional kerosene lamp gives a soft, cosy light and also radiates a little heat. There is always a risk with candles, but if supervised they create a soft and flickering light. Headlamps are perfect when you are upside down in the engine room or some small space. They provide light where you are looking and you have your hands free.

NIGHT LIGHT

White light disrupts night vision. If you are travelling with the boat at night, a diffuse red or green light, preferably LED, can provide a good guiding light.

COSY LIGHTING

Fitting light strips under the gunwale can provide pleasant ambient light. They light up the many dark corners on board.

NAVIGATION TABLE

A lamp on a flexi-arm is suitable for this, so that light can be directed where it is most needed. The light should be adjustable, to preserve night vision. There are also lamps with a detachable red filter, but a soft, white light is better to distinguish all the details on the charts.

DIMMER

Nowadays there are 12-volt (V) dimmer switches that can be used to regulate brightness – and save energy – for most types of lights (except fluorescent tubes). This makes it easy to adjust the brightness on a reading light, for example, and is nice when you have stopped reading but do not want total darkness. 12V dimmers cost from about £30.

5 TIPS FOR BETTER LIGHTING

1. Do not have all the light fitments attached to the cabin ceiling.

2. Have more than one light source to enable you to vary the light according to need.

3. Upward lighting that falls onto the cabin ceiling can create a softer ambient light.

4. A spotlight on a picture, for example, can create interesting light and make the boat feel more spacious.

5. Do not skimp on good-quality light sources.

SMART FAN FROM COMPUTER PARTS

A few pieces of wood trim and an old fan for a PC were turned into an energy-efficient fan to mount at the head-end of the berth. It will provide much needed cool air on still summer nights.

On hot summer nights it can be quite muggy when you try to sleep, especially when the boat has absorbed the heat of the sun during the day. But a small, quiet and fairly low-energy PC fan can create enough air circulation to make it feel cool and comfortable to sleep in.

If you have both the fan and the wood trim to surround it at home, it can be a very cheap or even cost-free project!

OBSOLETE PC PARTS

This project is based on parts taken from a discarded PC (ours had been gathering dust in a wardrobe for many years). We used the fan from the power unit, but chassis or graphics card fans can also be used, if the diameter is large enough.

Two common fan sizes are 8 cm (3 in) and 12 cm (5 in) diameter; the bigger the fan, the more effectively it will whirl the air round the sleeper.

This small and inexpensive fan provides low-energy cooling on hot summer days on board the project boat Roobarb.

A dusty old fan from an obsolete PC was the starting point for building the fan for Roobarb.

113

In this case the fans use about 0.2 A and have ball bearings. They are virtually silent, with a noise level of less than 10–20 dBA (see box on page 115 for terminology). If you want, you can add a small rheostat to regulate the speed.

MATERIALS

A new PC fan costs £10–20. Choose one that is both silent and has the largest possible airflow (about 25 CFM is common, but over 50 is very good).

Teak, mahogany, oak, or perhaps birch trim can be bought from a well-stocked timber yard. We had problems finding a suitable material at the builders' merchants, but we found some teak trim that was fine in a small timber yard near Stockholm.

This plastic fan only cost £5, but does not go with the interior quite as well as our home-made fan with the teak frame.

1

▲ The old fan is cleaned with compressed air and tested with a 12V source to see whether it still works properly.

2

▲ The trim is cut to fit the outer dimensions of the fan to become a deep box that covers the front.

3

▲ The frame of teak trim is glued together to fit round the PC fan. Other types of wood can be used to suit the boat interior.

4

▲ We found some materials for the project at the builders' merchants, although not all we needed.

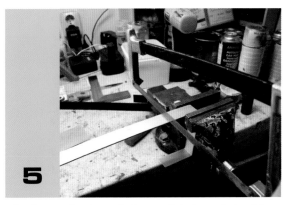

5

▲ A mounting is made from a flat piece of aluminium, which is easy to bend to shape.

6

▲ The frame is glued together and sanded, first with a machine and then by hand.

7

▲ A coat of varnish is applied after de-greasing the teak with acetone or methylated spirit.

8

▲ Placed over the berth, the fan is easy to direct onto the head or body, whichever you prefer.

Terminology on board

Noise level is measured in decibels (dB), the unit used to measure the intensity of sound waves, i.e. the effect per area. 0 dB is the lowest sound that a human ear can hear and 30 dB represents a whisper at a metre's distance. The unit dBA stands for sound pressure within acoustics, and how humans perceive the sound.

Airflow is measured in cubic feet per minute (CFM), and 1 CFM equals 28.4 litres per minute = 0.47 cubic metre per hour. A common value of airflow in a PC is 25 CFM = 710 litres per minute = 12 cubic metres per hour.

PROJECT LOG

SKILL LEVEL: easy.
TIME: 2 hours.

115

06
THE COCKPIT

>> SOFTER SEATING

Most of us spend long days in the cockpit, at least when the weather is good. A few minor improvements can make life on board more comfortable.

When you are sailing, you often spend many hours in the cockpit in all kinds of weather. It is easy to get a sore behind after a while! Waterproof cushions are one way of making days at sea more comfortable.

Many of us still use conventional kapok cushions. Very faded after the summer and often a bit damp from the latest shower, it is like sitting down on a barely squeezed sponge.

Americans know about comfort. For many years now they have had practical, waterproof cushions made of plastic with closed cells. This means they do not absorb any water; but they can also be quite hard to sit on.

The company BottomSiders, based in Washington in the US, uses a cell plastic material called Ensolite, which they coat with several layers of liquid UV-resistant vinyl. The vinyl creates a uniform, wipeable surface, available in nine colours. Boatbuilders Hallberg-Rassy is one of their customers.

CUSHIONS

There are two obvious ways of avoiding damp cushions. One is to use a water-repellent material, like PVC-coated cloth, to protect the foam in the centre of the cushion from water. The other is to make sure the soft material in the cushion either cannot absorb any water at all, by having closed cells (Sensaten, Airgomma), or by virtually letting the water run straight through large open cells (Dryfeel, Ezidri, among others).

MAKE YOUR OWN CUSHIONS FOR THE COCKPIT

I cut out a comfortable, waterproof cushion to cover the whole cockpit during lazy, sunny days, or tropical nights when it is too hot to sleep below deck (the boat is for long-distance sailing). For ordinary active sailing, the cushions are only used on the benches. Then you have a warm and comfortable seat – even in the rain and cold.

The material we used for *Roobarb*'s cushions is a closed cell plastic material, which does not absorb any water at all. It is the same kind of material used for sleeping pads, but better quality.

The material Sensaten is harder than ordinary foam rubber and easiest to cut with a band saw or a sharp carpet knife. However, I successfully used the second-hand electric bread-knife that I had bought on the internet, even though the edges are not perfectly straight. It is possible to sand them down if they have to be perfect. If you need a large piece, it is possible to glue pieces with contact adhesive and press together.

Initially, I considered using the material as it was, as I liked the blue colour. There are several colours to choose from.

However, I was a bit concerned that it would be too sweaty to sit on, and therefore I picked a Teflon-coated fabric, which repels moisture and is UV-resistant. If you want to sunbathe on the cushions, you should also put a towel on them.

There are commercial versions on the market which use polyether foam rubber with large open cells (Dryfeel), where the water can run straight through, so that the cushion dries quickly.

The sleeping-pad-like material we used is called closed-cell foam. It comes in blocks of 1 x 2 m (3 x 6 ft), in various thicknesses from 5 mm (0.2 in) to 85 mm (3.3 in), and the colours yellow, blue, black and white. The material has good buoyancy and is often used as protection for packaging, against vibrations, and as insulation. It can be covered or used as it is.

I also made flat fenders out of this material for *Roobarb*.

PROJECT LOG

TIME: 4 hours.

SKILL LEVEL: easy to medium (if you sew the cushion covers).

TOOLS: a sharp knife or electric bread-knife.

▲ The cockpit can be measured the same way as for the cushions in the cabin – the more precise the template, the better, of course.

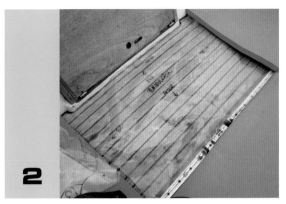

▲ The last piece under the bridge deck is measured. Later I moved the mainsheet track to a Targa frame.

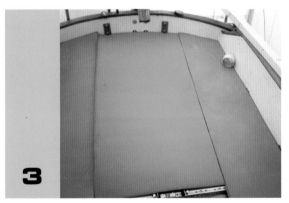

▲ An extra piece is made to cover the centre of the cockpit, so it can be used as a berth when you are in warm climates.

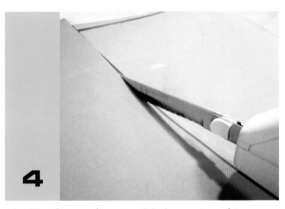

▲ Use the templates to minimise waste and to maximise the use of material. I used the electric bread-knife for cutting.

▲ The cushion fabric is Teflon-coated, can withstand sun and repels water, and is sewn like any other cushion cover. However, I used spray glue to attach the back of the cushion.

▲ The end result was tested during the winter, when the boat was still under protective cover.

SHAPABLE COCKPIT CUSHION

Perhaps you remember the beanbags or Sacco bags that were popular in the late 1970s. A shapeless sack on the floor filled with little plastic balls, which moulded to your body shape when you sat on them and sank into the filling.

These bags are also ideal for use on sailing boats that often lean to one side, and this can be a way of creating a very comfortable and warm seat almost anywhere on board. They are also common on extreme racing boats, which sail long distances; sitting for weeks on end in damp rain gear is not good for your behind and a beanbag can help to avoid nasty abscesses on your skin.

MAKE YOUR OWN

Use a strong, synthetic-coated canvas fabric and sew a rectangular sack with rounded corners, using strong double or triple seams. Stitch the rectangle inside out first, then turn it the right way out and sew another straight seam around the whole sack, leaving a 10-cm (4-in) opening. Depending on the material, you may have to lockstitch the fabric along the edges to prevent fraying.

Fill the sack to two-thirds with EPS-balls (I used approximately 25 litres/15.5 gal for mine). Stitch up the opening (I stitched on a handle at the same time) and possibly add a double seam across the middle of the sack, so that all the balls don't end up in one corner. This way you get a cushion to sit on and one for the back.

Expanded polystyrene (EPS)

Expanded polystyrene (EPS) beads can be bought in some DIY shops or, if asked, directly from the manufacturers. Because of their bulk, they can be difficult to send by mail. EPS is a closed-cell structure made of petroleum-based plastic that has been treated with steam to expand to more than 40 times its original size.

I managed to complete the whole cushion single-handedly, and found it very comfortable when I wriggled my rear into it.

1

▲ I sew a strong bag of a suitable size, with double seams. First, I stitch along the inside.

2

▲ Then I turn the bag the right way out and sew a second seam all the way round. I use strong synthetic thread designed for boat covers.

3

▲ The bag is filled to two-thirds with EPS-balls and then stitched by hand or on a machine.

4

▲ Finished, and very comfortable and warm to sit on.

The cushion is also ideal to sit a small child on – it stays comfortable and stable even when the boat heels.

>> OTHER COCKPIT PROJECTS

During the holiday, a lot goes on in the cockpit. This is where you want to socialise, perhaps invite new friends for dinner, and also be protected from the weather.

WIND SCREEN (DODGER)

A well-designed wind and water screen protects the crew in the cockpit against draughts and splashing waves, and is normally positioned between the stanchions closest to the cockpit. A good wind screen is one that can be rolled and tied up in really bad weather, so as not to act as an extra wind surface or be damaged if the waves roll in across the gunwale. A window makes it easier to see properly. It is also useful to stitch on pockets for storing things, from the sheet for the genoa track to the winch-winding gear.

A good spray dodger is a useful optional extra on a sailing boat. The one shown here is completely transparent, offering good visibility and protection at the same time.

Lennart Svensson's idea of having spray dodgers that can be rolled up is good when there are strong winds or high waves.

BARBECUE

This is another area where the Americans are a few steps ahead of us. A good barbecue, often LPG-powered, mounted on the pushpit, is a common feature of US boats. Grease and other debris from the barbecue land in the water, instead of on the deck (or rocks).

A home-made barbecue on board the OE32, made out of a stainless steel bowl and a round grill rack. The positioning reduces the risk of coals leaving burns on the boat or hot grease stains on the teak deck.

WINCH CAPS

Protect the expensive winches from dirt. Caps can be bought, but are not that hard to make. Fasten with rubber cord or attach a ribbon, so they do not get blown away.

BACK CUSHIONS

It's good to have some sort of cushioning on both the guardrails and the pushpit. These can also be bought, but are fairly easy to make.

Anyone who sails knows how uncomfortable the cockpit coaming can be, with the guardrail against your back. Many modern boats also have low coaming in the cockpit, which is not very comfortable for the back. The rolls in the picture (right), from Bedflex, open flat and are fastened with Velcro. The cushion (above) is from BottomSiders and is made to order to fit the cockpit shape.

123

SUNROOF/COCKPIT COVER

If you sail in warm waters, a sunroof or bimini top may be desirable to keep the sun off the cockpit. And a spacious cockpit tent makes it possible to use the cockpit even when low-pressure rains make life miserable.

PUSHPIT SEATS

These can be made out of steel or wood, or even strong textiles. The exact design depends on the shape of the pushpit and the available space. The more sophisticated come ready integrated into the pushpit structure.

Left: Sun screens come in different styles, from the simplest to specially made bimini tops.

Top left and right: Rail-mounted pushpit seats; the American seat on the left is cushioned for comfort. Bottom left: An aluminium kit from Noa can be adapted to suit most boats. Bottom right: A folding wooden seat on a Nauticat.

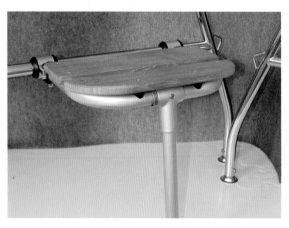

COCKPIT TABLE

A good table in the cockpit is ideal for dinner when moored. Different solutions for table legs can be invented, depending on the cockpit shape. The Lagun rotating table is a classic that fits almost all types of cockpit; now there is even one with a child-seat of the sort used on bicycles, so that small children also can enjoy the cockpit safely.

Top: A good cockpit table must be sturdy yet detachable, so you can have space to move around. Lennart has made a table top to fit the hatch for easy storage (above, left and right).

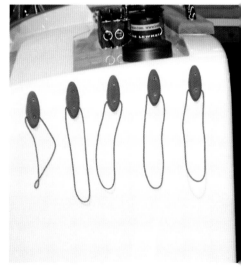

Right: A smart solution for tidying sheets in the cockpit and the storage of warps in a locker makes life aboard much easier in the long run.

>> A NEW NAME FOR THE BOAT

The boat's name on the transom stern or the hull sides looks good and gives the boat personality. There are different ways of making an attractive nameplate; we explored ordering pre-cut vinyl on the internet as a method of doing this.

Choosing the right name for the boat can sometimes be harder than naming your own children. Ideally it should be witty and fun and also convey something about the owner. Imagination has no limitations.

You should ideally mount the nameplate in a prominent place on the boat. There are various ways to do this, from carving a wooden nameplate to painting on the name.

The usual place is on the transom stern or somewhere on the hull side; in many places, there are certain rules for how the name should look or where it should be placed.

MADE TO ORDER OR HOME-MADE

The most common type of nameplate is made out of self-adhesive vinyl letters.

These can be produced in many ways, from making them from scratch to ordering on the internet.

Ordering from a website is a simple way of getting an attractive nameplate. You just enter the name of the boat and pick the font for the letters, choose the colour of the vinyl, and the plate size. A few days later a package turns up in the post and then you just go to the boat, clean the surface, and stick on the name somewhere suitable.

If you want to personalise it a little, you can make a design and send off the file for cutting. All the text and pictures must be vectorised, which can only be done in certain drawing programs, although the plate-making company can probably help out for a fee.

The best vector images are text, drawings and illustrations. Photos are difficult to get right, even if it is possible to a certain degree to convert them to one-colour, styled and vectorised pictures.

Adhesive vinyl comes in different qualities, defined by how long they are expected to adhere before falling off. A good vinyl quality is the one called 7 Year Vinyl, which is normally suitable for outdoor use and boats.

Seize the opportunity before the summer is upon you to make a new, personalised nameplate if the old one is beginning to fade. Let your imagination run wild!

PROJECT LOG

SKILL LEVEL: easy.

COST: approx. £20–40.

TIME: 30 minutes.

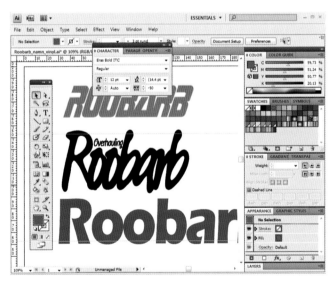

*I wanted to have my own design for the name of the project boat **Roobarb**, so I made it in the drawing program Adobe Illustrator, where I could easily try out different fonts.*

A close-up of the text, enlarged by 500%. The top line is bitmapped and the bottom line vectorised. The file names normally end in .ai .eps .cdr or sometimes .pdf. Use vector drawing programs, such as CorelDRAW or Adobe Illustrator.

If you are a real enthusiast, you can buy your own plotter. The smallest ones cost about £300 and are the same size as a standard desktop printer.

FOCUS ILLUSTRATION METHODS

You can make your own illustration from fonts, symbols and pictures cut out in vinyl. Here, I am sticking on the logo for the Biscay–Baltic cruise I did in a 6-metre (20-foot) centreboarder a few years back.

The result on the horseshoe buoy was good, although I should probably have picked a different colour that didn't merge with the dots on the Tiogruppen waxed cloth we used to cover the buoy.

Individual letters can be bought in a chandlery. Letters 50–75 mm (2–3 in) high can be screwed onto the deckhouse, or better still onto a piece of hardwood. Chromed brass is available from about £15 per letter.

I also tried making my own letters. First, I printed the letters in large scale on a printer. Step two was outlining the letters in reverse on the back of the vinyl backing. Finally, I cut them out.

Water-jet cut letters from stainless steel plate. To keep the price down you can polish them yourself, since it takes time.

Wood: carving a name into a piece of hardwood requires certain skills and/or patience. A simpler method is to use templates for the hand milling-machine to achieve neat letters (available from Biltema from £10).

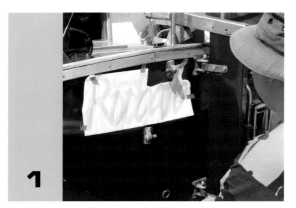

▲ The text was ordered from the internet. A couple of days later it arrives, covered with a protective film to ensure the letters stay in place when the backing is removed.

▲ I spray the hull with water with some washing up liquid, which will allow a little margin for adjustments.

▲ Holding the text by its protective film, I start to pull off the backing and carefully press on the first letter.

▲ With a foam spatula I smooth out the vinyl, starting in one corner to make sure any air pockets are squeezed out.

▲ Finally I peel back the film carefully, whilst checking that the vinyl stays firmly in place.

▲ The name of my home port is on the stern, looking very fine indeed.

REFERENCES

>> FACTS: PLYWOOD

Plywood, or cross-veneer as it used to be known, comes in thicknesses ranging from one to several millimetres, and consists of between three and twenty layers of crossed veneer of various kinds of wood. What to choose for the interior projects?

Plywood is by far the most common material in our boats, next to the hull's glass fibre reinforced plastic. It is incredibly versatile and can be used for almost the whole interior (or actually, to build the whole boat). The material is strong, easy to work with and cheap.

But you have to find the right plywood. It depends very much on what you are going to use it for. If it is for the interior and not the structure (i.e. main bulkhead, etc.), fairly basic plywood is adequate. If it is visible, the top veneer should be good and flawless. Simply speaking, the more thin layers there are in the plywood, the finer the quality.

IS IT HIGH-GRADE WOOD?
The top layer of mahogany plywood is roughly 0.5 mm (0.02 in) thick and 90% of the veneer is made of other, cheaper wood types. But it is still called mahogany plywood, even though only 1 mm out of 12 (0.05 in out of 0.5 in) is mahogany. The rest is probably some other African hardwood, such as lauan.

QUALITY
A standard board is 244 cm (8 ft) long and 122 cm (4 ft) wide. There are bigger boards available, which are the choice of boatbuilders to avoid having to join

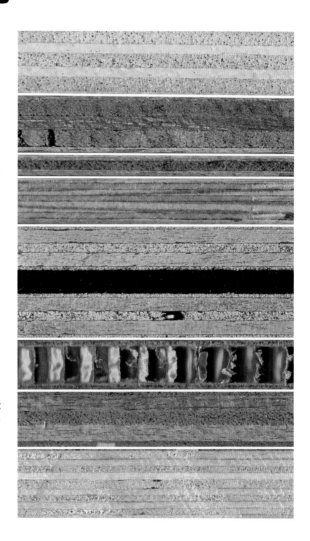

two boards together. The thickness varies, as does the number of layers.

The glue you want to use for boats is called weather- and water-boilproof, or WBP. It is a phenol resin adhesive that provides a brownish, waterproof glue line. Other adhesives may be called INT (interior glue) or MR (moisture-resistant). Both are less suitable for boats.

However, it is only the glue that is waterproof – wood always absorbs water and needs to be protected with other means.

TOP VENEER

At well-stocked timber yards you can find plywood with letter codes such as A/X, A/B, BB/C, etc. These indicate the veneer used in the surface layer. A is the best to be used in the saloon after varnishing. X is plywood that is not going to be seen.

Marine plywood is of exceptional quality and totally waterproof. It is made of pine, but also some purer grade woods. The veneer is glued together with no air pockets.

HOW CAN YOU ASSESS THE QUALITY?

One way of grading the quality of unmarked plywood is to look at the board from the side. If there are a lot of holes, the quality is lower. As mentioned earlier, the number of layers may also be an indication of the quality.

The top veneer may be cut with a knife (finest) or lathed. If it is important to have a perfect surface, then knife-cut or matched wood is best. Even plywood of the same material may vary in colour and structure. Read more about wood later on in this section.

It is hard to find good plywood, but it is available from some special timber yards or you can ask to buy some from a boatbuilder. Some major plywood suppliers unfortunately do not sell odd boards to private individuals.

TREATMENT

All visible plywood should be treated – up to 12 coats of varnish to get that perfect finish, which makes the wood surface look like it has been dipped in glass.

If better protection is needed, a two-component lacquer or epoxy can be used. Epoxy, however, is not as UV-resistant and should have a coat of protective

varnish if used outdoors. The edges in particular should be saturated with epoxy if the environment is at all damp.

DARKENED PLYWOOD

Most types of wood turn black when there is mould from water. It can be bleached out after the mould has been killed (for example, by applying the herbicide Boracol). The black will remain, but can be bleached a little. If you want a perfect finish, you have to re-veneer or replace the wood. Teak or khaya plywood (1.5 mm/0.06 in) is good for re-veneering.

Teak and mahogany veneer change colour with time, and it can be hard to match a new veneer. To a certain degree, you can varnish to achieve a better match.

SPECIAL PLYWOOD

Plywood is particularly well suited to creating materials for specific purposes. Lightweight plywood has a honeycomb centre of plastic or waxed board, to keep the weight down. It is used, among other things, in doors where the frame is of solid wood and the centre is of lightweight plywood.

There is also plywood with a layer of heavy bitumen in the centre, which is made for sound-proofing the walls of engine rooms, for example. Another type can be bent to a small radius.

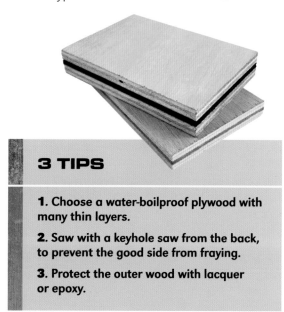

3 TIPS

1. Choose a water-boilproof plywood with many thin layers.

2. Saw with a keyhole saw from the back, to prevent the good side from fraying.

3. Protect the outer wood with lacquer or epoxy.

>> FACTS: FOAM RUBBER

Foam rubber gets old and loses its elasticity after a few years, but if you invest in quality it can take up to ten years before the bottom of the berth starts to feel hard through the sleeping pad. There are many different qualities and thicknesses in foam rubber pads. The most common in boats is a thickness of 5–10 cm (2–4 in). A thicker pad is firmer, not the opposite, as you might expect.

The firmness (density) of a pad can be important in withstanding spot loads, for example when you are lying on your side in the berth.

The foam density/volume weight (weight per cubic metre) is normally around 28–35kg/m3 and is available in both hard and soft versions.

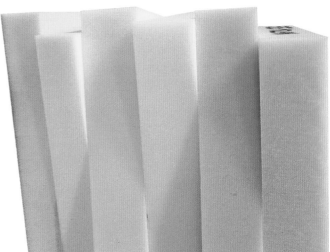

WHAT IS FOAM?

Different cell plastics or natural rubber are expanded by gas being introduced into the material, which is then heated and creates a large number of cavities. The cells can be open (soft, absorbent, used in pads, non-waterproof) or closed (waterproof, used for insulation or sleeping pads).

Open cell foam is usually made from polyester and the density is 18–110 kg/m³.

For boat pads, a polyether foam called cold foam (highly elastic and fireproof), with a density of 23–80 kg/m³, is normally recommended.

Latex, which is a natural material, is a little more expensive and suitable for really sensitive sleepers. Perhaps it is better in that case to opt for a sprung mattress, if you want the best. It builds more height than foam, about 15 cm (6 in) in total, and costs a bit more.

Density

Density indicates an object's mass per volume. It states how 'heavy' or 'light' something is.

Density is measured in kilograms per cubic metre (kg/m³).

RECOMMENDATIONS

Back support 5 cm (2 in) (density 28 kg/m³).

Seat pad 7–7.5 cm (3–3.2 in) (density 28 kg/m³).

Sleeping pad 10 cm (4 in) (density 35 kg/m³).

MEMORY FOAM

Memory foam can be used for a comfortable top mattress (or by itself in thicker models). The visco-elastic polyurethane foam is slow to regain its shape, so if you press your hand into the material and then release it, your handprint remains visible for several seconds. This property acts as pressure relief for the back, but may take some getting used to.

The material is expensive, although it has in recent years become cheaper, as more manufacturers have started using it. On board, it is mostly used for sleeping pads on top of harder seating pads in the saloon, to make them more comfortable to sleep on.

≫ FACTS: SPRAY GLUE

MINITEST: SPRAY GLUE FOR FOAM RUBBER

If you are gluing together a box of foam rubber boards around the steel springs when making a berth mattress, the glue is very important to the end result.

Having tested various spray glues, but also ordinary contact adhesive, I found two glues that work well, but unfortunately are hard to find.

The tests were carried out on test pieces of foam rubber and some of the tested glues – 3M Multimount and Danalim spray contact adhesive – are not at all suited to this type of gluing.

Ordinary solvent-based contact adhesive in a can/tube also works, but forms a stiff glued joint; however, it really keeps the pieces of foam rubber together and thus it does the job. Furthermore, this type of contact adhesive is easy to find in almost any hardware store.

THE BEST GLUE

The best results in my tests were the special glues Nevotex Comet and 3M FoamFast 74, both of which have excellent adhesion for foam rubber and other porous materials, but Nevotex was a cut above 3M.

Both spray cans have convenient nozzles with an adjustable spray range, so that you do not spray too much outside the intended area.

Both glues go a long way, but buy an extra can for each mattress, just in case.

Unfortunately, spray glue is not particularly health-friendly, and good ventilation is a must. According to the labels, they are only sold to the trade and can be hard to find, but are available online and in stores that sell foam rubber.

⟩⟩ FACTS: MULTI-PURPOSE SAWS

A Japanese saw is a practical tool for carpentry – easy to use, effective and an alternative to the keyhole saw in many cases. What makes it different from ordinary saws is that it cuts when you pull it towards you. That way the blade can be much thinner, resulting in a finer cut.

Most of us have used an ordinary saw that makes the cut when you push it away from you. The metal must be strong, so that the blade does not bend and break, whereas a Japanese saw can have a very thin blade, since it makes the cut as is it pulled towards you.

I read somewhere that someone had compared the Japanese saw to a simple piece of string – it is straight when you pull it towards you, but if you try to push it away, it is tricky and it bends! You can say the same thing about how a Japanese saw cuts a piece of wood when pulled towards you.

PRACTICE MAKES PERFECT

A certain amount of practice is required to cut neatly with the Japanese saw, but after a while it is no more difficult than using an ordinary saw. The handle, of plastic or bamboo, is often completely straight with space for two hands, like a Japanese sword. But these saws are also available with the grip we are used to. The main advantage with a Japanese saw is that the cutting line is finer and less

material is lost. The teeth are honed on three sides to make them extremely sharp. The blade is very thin – some parts can be a fraction of a millimetre. It makes the saw very agile, but it is also easier to bend the blade if you enter at an angle. After some practice it is incredibly fast.

TYPES OF SAW

The type of Japanese saw most commonly found is the 'double model', with double sides and teeth in both directions. Some of these saws have one side with Japanese teeth for cutting across the grain, while the other side has ordinary teeth, which are better for cutting along the grain.

The thinner the blade, the more support is needed for the saw's back. Therefore many of the very fine-toothed saws have a support across the back to make it more stable.

On some saws, the front part of the blade is unsupported, so you can bend the saw if you need to cut very close to something.

I tested different materials, from easy-to-cut pine and plywood, to medium density fibreboard (MDF), to hard, and difficult-to-cut, oak.

I also tried to cut a longer piece with a small hand saw and with a Japanese saw – neither cut perfectly straight, but the Japanese saw was easier to use and more effective.

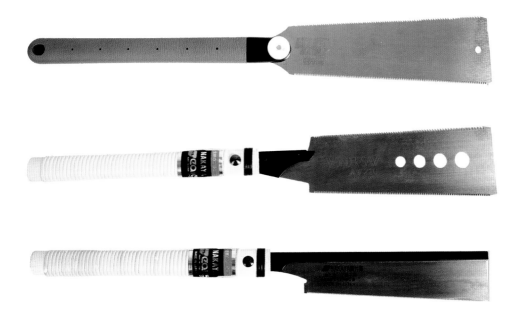

THE RESULT

The Japanese saw was a nice surprise for me. To start with, I tried to press too hard and the blade stuck and bent. But as soon as I learned to let the saw do the work, it went better. After a while I learned how much pressure I could apply and I quickly sawed long pieces. Now I often prefer the Japanese saw to the keyhole saw, for both small and big jobs.

At the boat shows there are always one or two sales representatives selling saws and demonstrating the efficiency on a piece of pine. Pine is one of the easiest wood types to cut.

When I tried sawing hard wood, I quickly realised that the Japanese saw is much harder to work with in that type of material. Of course the same applies to using a power keyhole saw or ordinary hand saw, so this was no real surprise.

I really recommend a Japanese saw for projects in your boat.

Top: This saw has an American-sounding name, but is made in Japan. Bear Saw BS250D is an all-purpose saw with a cutting side and a cleaving side. The rubber-clad handle gives a very good grip and it is easy to change blades. The saw comes with 22 teeth/30 mm (1.2 in) and a 0.5 mm (0.02 in) thick blade. (Bear Saw BS250D from Vaughan.)

Centre: The all-purpose saw is a combined cutting and cleaving saw, with two sides where the cutting side has Japanese honing and the cleaving has normal teeth. If you are a novice at using Japanese saws, then this is a good saw. The blade is 0.4 mm (0.16 in) thick and has 23 teeth/30 mm (1.2 in) on the cutting side. (Wonder Saw 220 from Nakaya.)

Bottom: The Japanese saw with the thinnest blade that we tested. This requires a little experience, as it is easy to break the saw: it makes very fine cutting lines with a 0.2 mm (0.008 in) thick blade and 36 teeth/30 mm (1.2 in). (Super Fine Cut 210 from Nakaya.)

>> FACTS: WOOD

Many types of wood can be used in the boat. Some are better suited than others to withstand damp and wear and tear. This is a brief overview of the most common types of wood you find at the timber yards or the carpenter.

Let us start by looking at the most commonly used types of wood in leisure boats. Traditionally, mahogany has been the standard, and for many the only option. And mahogany is a very suitable high-grade wood with properties that make it ideal for boats.

The problem with many high-grade woods is that the harvesting of some is now a threat to the world's ever-decreasing rainforests, which currently represent about 7% of all forest.

Some suppliers of high-grade wood mark their timber with so-called FSC certificates to indicate where the wood comes from and if it has been cultivated. Read more in the facts box.

As the high-grade woods are slowly disappearing from the market, boatbuilders try to find alternatives. The French yards especially have come far and are now using new wood types in their interiors, in particular cherry.

When it comes to the weight of different woods, it varies depending on whether it is heartwood or splintwood, is close-grained or has big gaps between the annual rings. The weights quoted in the fact boxes are average weights.

Many of the woods are also available as cross-veneer/plywood (see the section about plywood).

FSC CERTIFICATION
FSC stands for the Forest Stewardship Council, and since 1993 it has pioneered a voluntary environmental certification scheme. This is intended to prevent illegal deforestation and to promote responsible forest management, where trees are only harvested to alleviate the pressure on demand for threatened species such as mahogany and teak. The rights of indigenous populations are also respected.

FSC is backed by non-governmental organisations (NGOs) including WWF, Greenpeace and the Woodland Trust, and there are national working groups in more than 50 countries, including the UK.

Unfortunately, it is not difficult to buy unmarked high-grade wood, and major Swedish boatbuilders still use teak and mahogany from rainforests.

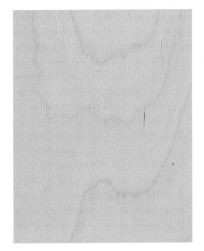  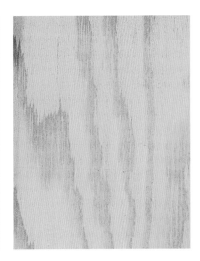

BIRCH (*Betula*)
Suitability for use in boats: ✳✳

Birch is a 10–20 m (32–65 ft) tall tree with a whitish bark with darker spots.

In total there are 40 types of birch; in Scandinavia, glass and wart birch are the most common, while in the UK silver and downy birch are prevalent, although not very suitable for use as timber. The colour of the wood is a pale red or yellowish white, where the annual rings are faint. Birch is a relatively heavy, hard and strong wood, but the resistance to rot is poor. It can easily be moistened with steam (bent), used for laminating, and glued.

Suitable for plywood.
Weighs approx. 660 kg (1455 lb)/m³.

BEECH (*Fagus sylvatica*)
Suitability for use in boats: ✳✳✳

Beech is a tall, summer green tree (30–40 m/100–130 ft) with a straight trunk and grey bark. The crown is dense and very leafy. The wood is pale brown to slightly reddish. Easy to bend with steam, it moves when it dries and buckles easily. A hard wood, with poor resistance to rot and insects. Easy to work with tools and to glue, it should be pre-drilled when screwed to avoid cracking.

Suitable for laminating (moisten with steam) and used primarily for furniture and interiors. Also available in plywood. It is also known as red beech.

Weighs approx. 720 kg (1585 lb)/m³.

PINE (*Pinus sylvestris*)
Suitability for use in boats: ✳✳✳✳

Pine is a 20–30 m (65–100 ft) tall tree that can be up to 900 years old. The pine tree has long needles in pairs. The colour of the wood is yellowish white when the timber is just planed, and becomes a darker yellow with time, while the heartwood becomes a darker reddish brown.

Pine is a soft wood, which is relatively resistant in relation to its density. The heartwood has annual rings close together and is fairly rot-resistant. It tends to have knots that can develop cracks and make it difficult to work with the material.

Suitable for interior plywood and building material.

Weighs approx. 450–500 kg (990–1200 lb)/m³.

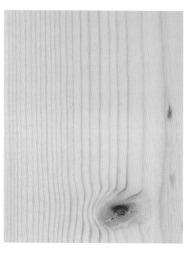

OAK (*Quercus roba*)
Suitability for use in boats:
*****

Oak is a large tree that grows to up to 20–25 m (65–80 ft). The bark, which is coarse, is pale grey and cracked and the tree often has a big crown. It can get very old – in fact, the oldest plant in the world is a 13,000 year-old oak in California.

The wood is heavy, hard and strong. The heartwood is light brown to brown and very rot-resistant. The splintwood is less rot-resistant. Oak is suitable to moisten with steam and perfect for frame ribs in wooden boats. However, all contact with iron should be avoided.

Oak is also easy to glue.

The hardness of the wood makes it difficult to work in and a hard-metal cutter is recommended.

Suitable for frame ribs, tables and interiors. Available in plywood.

Weighs approx. 720 kg (1585 lb)/m³.

FIR/SPRUCE (*Picea abies*)
Suitability for use in boats:
****

The fir tree or spruce is tall and straight and can grow to 60 m (200 ft) in height. The bark is thin and smooth and greyish or reddish brown. The needles are short and dark green.

The wood is paler than pine and yellowish white.

It is a soft, tenacious and pliable wood, with good rot-resistance.

The white wood is full of knots and must be treated with shellac if the surface is to be painted, to prevent the resin from discolouring the painted surface.

Fir is easy to work with tools and to glue. Douglas fir is a similar wood.

Suitable for plywood and masts, oars and hulls.

Weighs approx. 430 kg (950 lb)/m³.

IROKO (*Chlorophora excelsa*)
Suitability for use in boats:
***

The African iroko is really two closely related rainforest species. The tree is 40–45 m (130–150 ft) tall with a diameter of 0.7–1.7 m (2.3–5.6 ft). The wood is gold to dark brown and the heartwood is very rot- and insect-resistant, even though it cannot withstand cold that well. It is easy to work with tools and to glue and quite good for bending (moisten with steam). The negative features of iroko are a certain fragility and that it easily becomes discoloured by damp and metal.

Suitable for interiors, table tops and floorboards.

Similar wood to teak, iroko is sometimes called 'budget teak'. Can be used as an alternative to teak, but does not possess the same weather-resistant properties. Also known as 'African teak'.

Weighs approx. 640 kg (1400 lb)/m³.

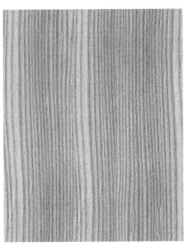

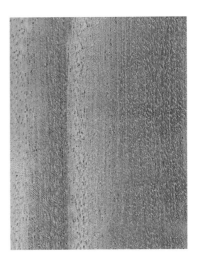

CHERRY (*Prunus avium*)
Suitability for use in boats: ***

Cherrywood comes from many closely related trees. The most common variety is sweet cherry or American black cherry. The colour is pale yellow to pale reddish brown, often with a pattern. American cherrywood is generally darker. It is a hard wood, easy to work with tools, to steam and to glue.

Suitable for veneer in plywood and becoming more popular in boat interiors with the big boatbuilders.

Weighs approx. 580–610 kg (1280–1345lb)/m³.

LARCH (*Larix decidua*)
Suitability for use in boats: *****

Larch is a fast-growing and thick deciduous tree that grows up to 35 m (115 ft) tall and sheds its needles in the autumn.

The wood is called larch or larchwood; it is similar to pine, and reddish brown, elastic and very rot-resistant.

The distinguishing feature of larch is that it is mainly heartwood; splintwood is often only about 1 cm (0.5 in) wide.

Larch is a close relative of the spruce.

Suitable for use in boat hulls and decks. Available in plywood.

Similar wood to Siberian larch, pine and spruce.

Weighs approx. 590 kg (1300 lb)/m³.

MAHOGANY (*Swietenia mahagoni*)
Suitability for use in boats: ****

Mahogany is a tall tree, about 30–50 m (100–165 ft), and originates from South America and Cuba, but closely related woods can also be found in Africa. 'Real' mahogany from South America and Cuba is rare nowadays, but other close relatives of the mahogany family are also sold as mahogany. There are also examples of completely different wood types that the timber yards sell under the name 'mahogany'.

Mahogany is a very hard, solid wood, whose colour ranges from golden brown to dark red. It is relatively easy to glue and to work with tools.

Suitable for use in interiors and for table tops, deckhouses, etc. Available in plywood. Can be discoloured and damaged by damp.

Similar woods are khaya/African mahogany, sapeli, gabon, sipo, araputanga, etc.

Weighs approx. 540–640 kg (1190–1410 lb)/m³.

MERANTI/LAUAN (*Shorea pauciflora*, etc.)
Suitability for use in boats: ✳✳✳✳

Meranti is a family of trees, all from rainforests. The wood is classed depending on colour, and there is dark red, red, yellow, and white meranti, of which the dark red is the best for boat-related carpentry. The dark red is the heaviest, strongest and most rot-resistant variety. In total there are about 150 types of meranti relatives, of which 15 are classed as dark red meranti. It can be worked with tools, but is not easy to bend through steaming.

Suitable for interiors and outdoor. Usually found as top coat in cheap plywood. Also known as lauan.

Weighs approx. 670 kg (1480 lb)/m^3.

OREGON PINE (*Pseudotsuga menziesii*)
Suitability for use in boats: ✳✳✳✳

Oregon pine is also known as Douglas fir, but is neither pine nor fir. It grows in North America and can be up to 100 m (330 ft) tall with a diameter of almost 5 m (17 ft). Usually, though, it is about 40–60 m (130–200 ft) tall with a diameter of 0.9–1.8 m (3–6 ft). Forty years ago the whole load of a truck could be just one tree but they are smaller now. The wood is yellowish brown and easy to work with – like pine, it is easy to glue and screw. Suitable for boat decks and in plywood.

Weighs approx. 530 kg (1170 lb)/m^3.

TEAK (*Tectona grandis*)
Suitability for use in boats: ✳✳✳✳✳

Teak can grow up to 40 m (130 ft) tall, with a trunk radius of several metres. The fresh timber is greenish yellow, but darkens to a dark reddish brown. Teak is very hard, heavy, flexible and oily. The wood has a good resistance to rot and insects. The natural oil content means it does not need to be treated to be weatherproof. However, the same oiliness makes it hard to glue.

The high content of ingrained silica wears heavily on the tools when working with the material, and it is advisable to use a hard-metal cutter that is changed/honed often.

Pre-drill before screwing.

Suitable for boat decks and for both indoor and outdoor carpentry. Available in plywood.

Weighs approx. 650 kg (1430 lb)/m^3.

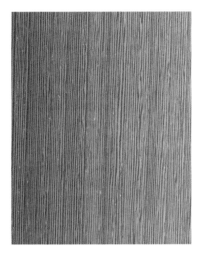

WALNUT (*Juglans regia*)
Suitability for use in boats: ✳✳

Walnut is a family of different woods from many places around the world – European, American and South American walnut are the most common.

Walnut is a large tree, about 25–30 m (80–100 ft) tall. The kernel of the well-known fruit, the walnut, is normally cracked at Christmas.

European walnut has a greyish-brown to brown colour wood with irregular darker stripes. American walnut is an even dark brown, sometimes with a hint of purple. It is medium hard and sensitive to pests. Easy to bend and to work with tools.

Suitable for veneer for carpentry as it is very expensive.

Weighs approx. 640 kg (1410 lb)/m³.

WENGÉ (*Milletia laurentii*)
Suitability for use in boats: ✳✳✳

The name 'wengé' originates from a local language of Congo-Kinhansa and the tree grows to about 30 m (100 ft) tall with a trunk diameter of 70–80 cm (28–32 in). The very heavy heartwood is dark brown with white or purple tones and often has a coarse surface. The beautiful dark brown colour fades quickly in sunlight and it is best used below deck.

Wengé is a strong, solid wood with extreme durability and resistance to insects and rot. Fairly easy to work with tools and to polish to an excellent finish.

Not suitable to bend. Pre-drill for screwing. Use gloves when handling, as splinters can cause inflammation.

Suitable for carpentry below deck.

A similar wood is panga-panga, a close relative.

Weighs approx. 830–1000 kg (1830–2200 lb)/m³.

Bamboo is being introduced as a material in boats, as it is very resistant to water and is hard and tenacious. Bamboo is actually not a wood, but a fast-growing grass.

Sources: *National Encyclopedia, World Woods in Colour* by William A. Lincoln. With help from Roine Falk and Nilsson Trävaror.

>> FACTS: INSULATION MATERIALS

INSULATION BOARDS

Insulation boards, such as Ecoprim 200, Thermisol F300, Floormate, or Styrofoam (pink or blue ground insulation board), are used for cold store insulation or ground insulation, among other things.

Glue with solvent-free (water-based) contact adhesive or polyurethane or epoxy glue, if you need strong joints. You can also use ordinary wood glue.

Made from extruded polystyrene cell plastic (XPS). Available from builders' merchants – not always in the big stores. The boards are sold individually and typical thicknesses are 20–100 mm (0.8–4 in).

Styrofoam is sold in large packs at places like Bauhaus, but these can be a bit too much for a small cool box. You can also buy it as individual boards.

FOAM

A simple material to use is some kind of polyurethane jointing foam, which, together with moisture (water), expands to twice its volume. Therefore, you must have pre-drilled holes where excess foam can flow through. Remove with a knife when it has hardened, after an hour or so.

Vacuum panel from Glacier Bay.

The disadvantage with jointing foam is that, after hardening, moisture can be absorbed and after a few years it can lose its insulating properties. It is easy to work with, as it automatically fills all available space. Some foam types contain iso-cyanates.

Extruded polystyrene has excellent insulation.

CELL PLASTIC (FRIGOLITE)

Frigolite is a closed cell plastic and is therefore suitable as insulation material. However, the insulation capacity is not as good as for ground insulation boards, which is why it is better to choose these. They are cheap and easy to find at the builders' merchants.

VACUUM PANELS

Ultra-R is a material originally made for NASA. Panels with vacuum provide good insulation capacity and you only need a tenth of the thickness compared to ordinary insulation material.

I wanted to use this material, but it was too expensive for me to import (over £1000 for the customised boards I needed). The panels must be made to order because of the vacuum, and they cannot be cut or drilled.

A version available in Sweden is Vacupor, which consists of a material called 'fumed silica'. It is a microporous material, which has been vacuum-sealed with metal foil to form boards. These boards cannot be cut or drilled. The panels come in different sizes

Frigolite, or cell plastic, has been around for many years. It is an adequate insulation material.

from 60 x 25 cm/24 x 10 in (cost about £28 for 20 mm/0.8 in thickness) but can also be made to measure. So far, the material has not been used to make a cool box for a boat.

Jointing foam is good for filling cavities and thus improving existing insulation.

Bubble plastic with foil can provide very good insulation, although no independent test results have been published.

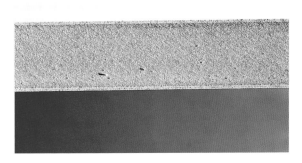

The material in these boards is from Isotherm and made of 47 mm (1.8 in) polyurethane, which has excellent insulation properties.

THERMOREFLECTANCE

Polynum Big is air-filled bubble plastic laid between two layers of reflective foil. According to the manufacturer, it has very good insulating properties and a high R-value, even though the basis for calculating the insulation capacity has been questioned by many. There are no independent studies.

Thermoreflectance needs an air column in order to insulate. I will insulate the deckhouse and the inside of the hull on *Roobarb* with this material, which I have already bought, instead of using it around the cool box.

ISOTHERM

Isotherm insulation boards are coated in plastic on both sides and consist of 47 mm (1.8 in) polyurethane with 2.5 mm (0.1 in) plastic material on both sides. This is the most readily available insulation material there is, since it is often stocked in chandleries. The boards are 978 x 478 x 50 mm (39 x 19 x 2 in) and come in packs of three.

>> INDEX